The Algorithmic Era - Living with AI in Every Day Life

Hasan Kamal

Published by Ink Freedom Publication, 2024.

The Algorithmic Era: Living with AI in Everyday Life

2

Hasan Kamal
Ink Freedom Publication
Qazi Street, Moradabad, Uttar Pradesh, 244001
www.inkfreedompublication.com
inkfreedompublication@gmail.com
+91 7452903706

Disclaimer

This book has been published with all reasonable efforts taken to make the material error-free after the consent of the author. No part of this book shall be used, reproduced in any manner whatsoever without written permission from the author, except in the case of brief quotations embodied in critical articles and reviews. The Author of this book is solely responsible and liable for its content including but not limited to the views, representations, descriptions, statements, information, opinions and references. The Content of this book shall not constitute or be construed or deemed to reflect the opinion or expression of the Publisher or Editor. Neither the Publisher nor Editor endorse or approve the Content of this book or guarantee the reliability, accuracy or completeness of the Content published herein and do not make any representations or warranties of any kind, express or implied, including but not limited to the implied warranties of merchantability, fitness for a particular purpose. The Publisher and Editor shall not be liable whatsoever for any errors, omissions, whether such errors or omissions result from negligence, accident, or any other cause or claims for loss or damages of any kind, including without limitation, indirect or consequential loss or damage arising out of use, inability to use, or about the reliability, accuracy or sufficiency of the information contained in this book.

About the Book

The Algorithmic Era: Living with AI in Everyday Life explores the deep, often invisible ways that artificial intelligence integrates into our daily lives, shaping our choices, interactions, and even identities. This book illuminates how AI has moved from the realms of labs and tech conferences into our personal routines and societal structures, subtly influencing everything from our shopping preferences to our health care experiences. Readers will journey through AI's role in personalizing our digital spaces, balancing privacy with convenience, and transforming workplaces and educational settings. With AI-driven platforms offering adaptive learning, automation reconfiguring industries, and smart technology making homes and cities "intelligent," our world is becoming more seamlessly connected yet poses new ethical challenges. The book also examines AI's impact on relationships, where social algorithms shape human interactions, and healthcare, where machine intelligence is advancing diagnostics and treatment. Addressing issues of bias, privacy, and responsibility, *The Algorithmic Era* critically considers the long-term societal implications of a world increasingly reliant on AI, challenging readers to consider what it means to live alongside intelligent systems and the ethical considerations of this transformation. Designed for general readers intrigued by the future of technology and social change, this book provides accessible yet thought-provoking insights into the ways AI will continue to reshape our lives and the choices we face in this new, algorithm-driven world..

Chapter 1. Introduction to the Algorithmic Era

Artificial Intelligence (AI) has transformed from a speculative idea into a powerful force embedded in nearly every aspect of modern society. In this opening chapter, we examine how AI has become a pervasive part of everyday life, influencing how we communicate, work, learn, and live. We'll also trace AI's journey from theoretical constructs to practical applications, exploring the rapid developments that have brought us into this new era. Finally, we'll consider the intricate interplay between AI technology and human routines, highlighting the profound ways in which AI is redefining the human experience.

Understanding AI's Impact on Modern Life

AI's influence on modern life is both subtle and sweeping. It has woven itself into the fabric of our daily activities, often without us even noticing. Think about how your day begins: an AI-powered virtual assistant might wake you up, followed by an algorithmic curation of news stories tailored to your preferences. As you commute to work or school, navigation apps powered by AI optimize your route, taking into account real-time traffic conditions. At work, AI tools may assist you in drafting emails, analyzing data, or automating repetitive tasks, increasing efficiency and reducing human error.

In entertainment, streaming platforms like Netflix or Spotify rely on AI algorithms to recommend content based on your viewing or listening habits, making your experience more engaging and personalized. But AI's reach extends beyond convenience and entertainment. In healthcare, AI models are revolutionizing how diseases are diagnosed and treated, often predicting medical outcomes with incredible accuracy. For example, AI can analyze medical images, detect anomalies, and assist doctors in making life-saving decisions. In agriculture, AI-driven systems optimize crop yields, while in finance, algorithms manage investments and detect fraudulent activities.

Despite these benefits, the widespread use of AI has raised significant concerns. Privacy is a major issue, as AI systems often rely on vast amounts of personal data to function effectively. The question of who controls this data and how it is used remains a hot topic of debate. Additionally, AI's ability to automate tasks has led to fears about job displacement, with certain industries already seeing a shift from human labor to AI-driven processes. Moreover, the ethical implications of AI decision-making—such as bias in algorithms or the lack of transparency in automated systems—demand serious consideration.

The Evolution of Artificial Intelligence

The story of AI's evolution is a tale of relentless innovation punctuated by moments of frustration and triumph. It began in the 1950s, with early pioneers like Alan Turing and John McCarthy laying the conceptual groundwork for machines that could think and learn. Turing's famous "Turing Test" questioned whether a machine could exhibit behavior indistinguishable from a human, sparking decades of research into replicating human intelligence. McCarthy later coined the term "artificial intelligence" and organized the Dartmouth Conference in 1956, a landmark event that aimed to explore the possibilities of machine-based reasoning.

The early years of AI research were full of ambitious promises, but progress was slow due to limitations in computing power and data availability. The field experienced several "AI winters," periods when funding and interest waned because expectations were not met. Yet, AI persisted, evolving through different paradigms. The development of expert systems in the 1970s and 1980s marked a new chapter, as researchers created rule-based systems that could perform tasks like diagnosing diseases or making financial forecasts. However, these systems were rigid and lacked the ability to learn from new data.

It wasn't until the 21st century that AI began to experience rapid growth, thanks to three key factors: the explosion of big data, advancements in computing power, and breakthroughs in machine learning algorithms. Deep learning, a subset of machine learning that uses neural networks to mimic the human brain, has driven many of AI's most impressive achievements. Technologies like natural language processing (NLP) and computer vision have enabled machines to understand and generate human-like text, recognize faces, and even beat human champions in complex games like go.

Today, AI has surpassed many of the limitations of its early years and continues to evolve at a breakneck pace. From autonomous vehicles to AI-powered customer service agents, the applications are vast and transformative. Yet, the rapid evolution of AI also brings new challenges. The question of how to regulate AI, ensure its ethical use, and prevent its potential misuse remains at the forefront of societal concerns.

The Intersection of Technology and Daily Living

The intersection of technology and daily living has never been more intertwined, largely due to the omnipresence of AI. In our homes, AI-powered devices like smart thermostats, lights, and security systems create a more efficient and secure living environment. These systems learn from our behavior, adjusting settings automatically to maximize comfort and minimize energy consumption. For instance, a smart thermostat may learn your schedule and ensure the house is warm when you wake up and cool when you leave for work, all without manual input.

AI also transforms how we communicate and form relationships. Social media platforms, governed by complex algorithms, curate our news feeds, prioritize content, and even suggest connections. While these algorithms can enhance engagement, they also come with drawbacks, such as the creation of echo chambers where opposing viewpoints are rarely seen. This can contribute to social polarization and a distorted perception of reality. Additionally, the use of AI in content moderation raises questions about censorship and the ability of algorithms to understand context and nuance.

In the professional sphere, AI has become a critical tool for optimizing workflows and enhancing productivity. In offices, AI software manages meeting schedules, prioritizes tasks, and even drafts reports. Industries like manufacturing use AI-driven robots to automate assembly lines, leading to faster production with fewer errors. However, this raises significant concerns about the future of work and the potential for widespread job losses, especially in roles that involve repetitive or manual tasks. The idea of human-AI collaboration, where AI enhances rather than replaces human capabilities, is gaining traction, but it requires careful planning and ethical considerations.

The influence of AI doesn't stop there. In education, AI-driven platforms provide personalized learning experiences, adapting to a student's pace and understanding. In healthcare, AI not only assists in diagnosing illnesses but also helps in developing personalized treatment plans. The intersection of AI and daily living presents a future full of possibilities but also a need for thoughtful regulation to ensure these technologies are used responsibly and ethically.

Summary of Chapter 1

This comprehensive introduction to *The Algorithmic Era* sets the stage for understanding the pervasive role of AI in our lives. By exploring AI's multifaceted impact, its historical evolution, and its integration into daily routines, we gain a clearer picture of how technology shapes the modern world. The journey of AI, from its humble beginnings to its current dominance, serves as a reminder of both the potential and the risks that come with such powerful tools. As we continue to engage with AI, it is crucial to be informed, aware, and prepared to make ethical decisions about its use and governance.

Chapter 2. AI in Everyday Routines: An Overview

Artificial Intelligence (AI) has seamlessly integrated into our daily lives, to the point where it influences many of our activities without us even realizing it. In this chapter, we will explore how AI algorithms are embedded everywhere, how they shape our behaviors and decisions as consumers, and how they simplify and enhance routine tasks. The deeper we go, the more we understand how much AI has redefined what it means to live in a technologically advanced world.

The Ubiquity of Algorithms

In today's world, algorithms are omnipresent. They operate behind the scenes, powering many of the digital tools and services we rely on. An algorithm, in simple terms, is a set of rules or instructions designed to solve problems or perform tasks. But when these algorithms are powered by AI, they can learn from data, adapt to changing inputs, and make decisions that influence our daily lives in profound ways.

From the moment we wake up and check our smartphones, algorithms start working. Social media platforms, such as Facebook, Instagram, and TikTok, use AI-driven algorithms to curate content for us. These algorithms analyze our behavior—what we like, share, or comment on—to create a personalized experience aimed at keeping us engaged for as long as possible. The same algorithms are used by search engines like Google, which rank search results based on a variety of factors, including relevance, user behavior, and content quality.

Email platforms also use AI algorithms. For instance, your email service automatically filters spam, moving unwanted messages to a separate folder based on learned patterns. News apps use algorithms to recommend articles that align with your interests, often creating a "filter bubble" that limits exposure to diverse perspectives. Even when you order food online, algorithms help suggest restaurants or dishes based on your past preferences.

But AI isn't confined to the digital world. It's in traffic management systems, where algorithms analyze real-time traffic data to optimize traffic lights and reduce congestion. It's in public transportation, helping to determine routes and schedules that maximize efficiency. Retail stores use predictive analytics to manage inventory, ensuring products are in stock when customers need them. Hospitals use AI systems to optimize patient care, from scheduling appointments to predicting patient needs.

The pervasiveness of these algorithms makes life more convenient and efficient, but it also raises ethical and philosophical questions. Who controls these algorithms? How much of our lives should be influenced by automated systems? And what happens when algorithms make mistakes or are biased? These are crucial considerations in an increasingly algorithm-driven society.

AI has revolutionized the way businesses interact with consumers. By leveraging vast amounts of data, AI-driven algorithms have made consumer experiences more personalized, efficient, and engaging. But this level of personalization comes at a cost, as AI also has the power to shape consumer behavior in ways that benefit corporations while subtly influencing our decisions.

Take online shopping as an example. E-commerce platforms like Amazon use AI to analyze you're browsing and purchase history, as well as the behaviors of similar users. With this data, AI algorithms generate personalized recommendations, showing you products you might be interested in and offering discounts designed to tempt you. This predictive power drives higher sales and enhances user satisfaction, but it also leads to impulsive buying and an environment where consumers are constantly pushed to spend more.

Streaming services like Netflix and Hulu use AI to analyze your viewing history and predict what you might want to watch next. These platforms aim to keep you engaged by auto-playing content and suggesting shows tailored to your interests. Similarly, music platforms like Spotify use AI algorithms to create personalized playlists, such as "Discover Weekly," which are generated based on your listening habits and preferences.

Targeted advertising is another area where AI's influence is strong. Advertisers use AI to identify potential customers and tailor ads to individual preferences. Have you ever noticed how ads for a product you recently searched for follow you across different websites? This is AI in action, using data from your browsing history to serve ads that are more likely to grab your attention. While these personalized ads can be useful, they also raise concerns about privacy and data security, as companies collect and store massive amounts of personal information.

Moreover, AI algorithms can influence consumer behavior by creating "echo chambers." By constantly presenting us with content that aligns with our existing preferences and beliefs, AI can limit our exposure to new ideas and reinforce our current opinions. This effect is not just confined to shopping and entertainment but extends to news consumption and social media interactions, where algorithms prioritize content that generates the most engagement.

The power of AI to shape consumer behavior has transformed marketing strategies and created a more tailored user experience. However, it has also sparked debates about data ethics, the psychological impact of constant recommendations, and the long-term consequences of a world where every consumer interaction is influenced by AI.

Routine Tasks Made Smarter

AI has significantly improved our ability to manage everyday tasks, making life more convenient and productive. From smart home devices to workplace automation tools, AI is changing how we handle routine activities. By learning our habits and preferences, AI-powered systems adapt to our needs and make real-time adjustments, creating a more efficient lifestyle.

Smart home technology is one of the most visible examples. Devices like smart thermostats, such as Nest, learn your temperature preferences and adjust settings automatically to ensure comfort while optimizing energy use. Smart lighting systems can be controlled through voice commands or programmed to turn on and off based on your daily schedule. Home assistants like Amazon's Alexa or Google Home can manage your to-do lists, set reminders, and even order groceries—all with simple voice commands. AI in the home extends to security as well. AI-powered cameras can recognize familiar faces, detect unusual activity, and alert homeowners if something seems amiss.

In the kitchen, AI is helping people become better cooks and manage their groceries more effectively. Smart refrigerators can monitor what's inside, alert you when food is about to expire, and even suggest recipes based on the ingredients available. AI ovens can adjust cooking times and temperatures for optimal results, while robotic kitchen assistants are being developed to prepare meals from scratch. These innovations save time and reduce food waste, making kitchens smarter and more efficient.

AI is also making waves in the workplace. Digital assistants handle tasks like scheduling meetings, prioritizing emails, and generating reports. AI-powered customer service chatbots can answer queries, book appointments, and assist customers 24/7, enhancing service while reducing the burden on human employees. In industries like manufacturing, AI-driven robots work alongside humans to assemble products, monitor quality, and even predict when equipment might fail, ensuring timely maintenance.

However, the convenience of AI comes with its own set of challenges. As we rely more on AI, there is a risk of losing basic skills, such as the ability to navigate without GPS or the patience to complete manual tasks. Moreover, the increasing dependence on AI raises security and privacy concerns. Many AI devices require access to sensitive data to function effectively, which could be vulnerable to hacking or misuse.

Despite these challenges, AI has undeniably made routine tasks smarter and our lives more efficient. The key is to find a balance between convenience and mindful use, ensuring that we retain control over these powerful tools while benefiting from the efficiencies they bring.

Summary of Chapter 2

This chapter delved into how AI has become an integral part of our daily routines. We discussed the pervasive nature of algorithms, the profound influence of AI on consumer behavior, and the ways AI has made routine tasks smarter and more efficient. While AI offers undeniable benefits in terms of convenience and personalization, it also poses ethical and security challenges that we must carefully navigate. As we continue to explore AI's role in our lives, understanding these dynamics will be crucial in harnessing its potential responsibly.

Chapter 3. The Personalization-Privacy Paradox

We live in an era where technology knows us better than ever before. From social media platforms to e-commerce websites, our online experiences are increasingly tailored to our preferences and habits, all thanks to artificial intelligence (AI). This personalization brings many conveniences but also raises significant concerns about privacy. The "Personalization-Privacy Paradox" is the struggle between enjoying customized digital interactions and the need to safeguard our personal data. This chapter delves deeply into the intricacies of this paradox, exploring the benefits and drawbacks of personalized experiences, the mechanics of the data economy, and the delicate balance between personalization and privacy rights.

Personalized Experiences: Benefits and Drawbacks

Personalization is a defining feature of our digital age. It's what makes our interactions with technology feel intuitive, relevant, and seamless. When you open your favorite music streaming app and find a playlist curated to your taste or receive shopping recommendations based on past purchases, you are experiencing the power of AI-driven personalization. These features are designed to make life more convenient and enjoyable, saving us time and effort by delivering what we want, often before we even know we want it.

Benefits of Personalized Experiences - The primary advantage of personalization is efficiency. Instead of sifting through endless options, we are presented with choices that align with our preferences. For example, personalized news apps prioritize articles that match our interests, keeping us informed on topics we care about most. Similarly, streaming services like Netflix and YouTube use sophisticated algorithms to suggest content that matches our viewing history, increasing user engagement and satisfaction.

Personalization also enhances e-commerce experiences. Online retailers use data from our browsing history, wish lists, and past purchases to recommend products we are more likely to buy. This can be incredibly useful when we're looking for a specific item or when we're open to discovering new things. Personalized ads and promotions can lead to better deals and more relevant shopping experiences. For businesses, the benefits are clear: personalization drives higher conversion rates, customer loyalty, and overall user engagement.

Drawbacks of Personalized Experiences - However, the benefits of personalization come with significant drawbacks. The same algorithms that make our lives easier also collect vast amounts of personal information, often without us fully realizing it. These systems track our online activities, monitor our interactions, and analyze our behaviors to build detailed profiles. This data is then used to make predictions about our future behavior, raising concerns about how much these companies know about us and what they do with that information.

One of the most troubling aspects of personalization is the potential for "filter bubbles" and "echo chambers." These occur when algorithms prioritize content that aligns with our existing views, limiting exposure to diverse perspectives. In the context of news and social media, this can reinforce biases, polarize opinions, and create a distorted sense of reality. Additionally, the feeling of being constantly monitored can be unsettling. Many people report feeling uncomfortable when they see ads or recommendations related to something they only casually mentioned or thought about, leading to concerns about digital surveillance.

Moreover, the push for personalized experiences can sometimes backfire. For instance, recommendations are not always accurate and may feel invasive or manipulative. There is also the risk of data breaches and misuse, as the more data companies collect, the greater the potential for that information to fall into the wrong hands.

The Data Economy and User Consent

At the heart of the personalization-privacy paradox is the data economy, a vast and complex ecosystem where personal data is the most valuable commodity. The data economy refers to the exchange of personal information for services, where companies collect and analyze user data to drive business decisions, target advertising, and refine their products. This economy is what enables many free services, such as social media platforms and search engines, to thrive. However, the methods used to collect and manage this data often lack transparency, making it difficult for users to understand the full scope of what they are consenting to.

How the Data Economy Works - When you use an app or browse a website, your data is being collected in real time. This can include everything from your location and browsing history to your preferences and social interactions. Companies use this data to create profiles, which are then analyzed to make predictions about your behavior and preferences. For instance, if an e-commerce platform knows that you recently searched for running shoes, it may show you ads for athletic apparel or related products on other websites. This type of data sharing and analysis fuels the digital advertising industry, which is a multibillion-dollar market.

Many companies also share or sell this data to third parties, such as advertisers, data brokers, or market researchers. This is where the concept of the data economy becomes murky. Users often have little understanding of who has access to their information and how it is being used. In many cases, data is collected and monetized in ways that are far from obvious, creating a sense of vulnerability among users.

The Issue of User Consent - User consent is supposed to be a safeguard that allows individuals to control how their data is used. When signing up for new services, users are often asked to agree to terms and conditions that outline data collection practices. However, these agreements are usually long and filled with legal jargon, making it unlikely that users will read or fully understand them. As a result, consent is often given without a true understanding of the implications.

The idea of "informed consent" is further complicated by the way data is collected passively. For example, apps may track your location even when you are not actively using them or monitor your online behavior across multiple devices. While some platforms have made efforts to be more transparent, many still do not offer clear explanations of their data practices. This lack of transparency and user control has led to widespread concerns about data privacy and the ethical responsibilities of companies in the data economy.

Governments and regulatory bodies have started to address these concerns. The European Union's General Data Protection Regulation (GDPR) and the California Consumer Privacy Act (CCPA) are examples of laws designed to give users more control over their data. These regulations require companies to be more transparent and give users the right to access, correct, or delete their data. However, implementing and enforcing these laws remains a challenge.

Balancing Personalization with Privacy Rights

Balancing the benefits of personalization with the right to privacy is one of the most pressing challenges in today's digital landscape. People enjoy the convenience of personalized services but are increasingly wary of the data collection practices that make these services possible. To address this paradox, various approaches are being explored, ranging from technological innovations to legal frameworks.

Transparency and User Control - One of the most effective ways to balance personalization and privacy is through increased transparency. Companies need to be upfront about what data they collect, why they collect it, and how it will be used. This transparency can empower users to make informed decisions about their data. Additionally, platforms should offer intuitive privacy settings, allowing users to customize their experience based on their comfort level. For example, some social media sites let users opt out of personalized ads or limit the amount of data they share.

User control is also critical. People should have the ability to easily access and manage their data, including options to delete or anonymize it. This is where privacy-enhancing technologies come into play. Encryption, for example, ensures that data is secure and accessible only to authorized parties. Anonymization techniques can remove personally identifiable information, allowing companies to use data for analysis without compromising user privacy.

Data Minimization and Ethical AI - Data minimization is a principle that suggests companies should only collect the data necessary to provide their services. By limiting data collection, the risk of breaches and misuse is reduced. For instance, a weather app should not need access to your entire contact list to provide accurate forecasts.

Companies that practice data minimization are more likely to earn user trust and reduce the impact of potential data leaks.

Ethical AI practices are another important component of balancing personalization and privacy. This involves developing algorithms that are not only effective but also fair and transparent. Companies should regularly audit their algorithms to ensure they do not reinforce biases or make decisions that unfairly impact certain groups. Ethical AI also includes giving users the option to understand how algorithms make decisions, especially in sensitive areas like credit scoring or job recruitment.

Regulatory Frameworks and the Role of Governments - Governments have a significant role to play in protecting user privacy while enabling innovation. Regulations like GDPR and CCPA set important precedents, but there is a need for more comprehensive and globally consistent data protection laws. These regulations should not only mandate transparency but also penalize companies that misuse or fail to protect user data. Collaboration between governments, tech companies, and privacy advocates is essential to develop balanced policies that respect user rights while fostering technological advancement.

Ultimately, finding the right balance requires a collective effort. Users must be proactive in protecting their data by understanding privacy settings and being cautious about what they share. Companies must prioritize ethical data practices and be transparent about their operations. Governments must enforce laws that hold organizations accountable while encouraging responsible innovation.

User Education and Awareness - Another critical factor in balancing personalization with privacy is educating users. Many people are unaware of the extent to which their data is collected or how it is used. Educational initiatives can help users understand the implications of sharing their personal information and how they can better protect their privacy. For instance, public awareness campaigns can teach people how to read privacy policies, adjust privacy settings, and recognize when apps are collecting unnecessary data. Schools and educational institutions could also include digital literacy and data privacy as part of their curriculum, preparing younger generations to navigate the digital world responsibly.

The Role of Privacy-First Companies - In response to growing privacy concerns, some companies are positioning themselves as privacy-first organizations. These companies prioritize user privacy by implementing strong data protection measures and offering services that do not rely on extensive data collection. For example, search engines like DuckDuckGo emphasize not tracking user activity, and messaging apps like Signal use end-to-end encryption to secure communications. The success of these privacy-first businesses demonstrates that it is possible to provide valuable services without compromising user privacy. Their practices set a benchmark for other companies and encourage a market where privacy can be a competitive advantage.

Technology and Innovation in Privacy Protection - Emerging technologies are also playing a role in protecting user privacy while still enabling some level of personalization. Techniques such as federated learning allow AI models to learn from user data without that data ever leaving the user's device. This reduces the risk of data breaches and enhances privacy. Differential privacy is another innovative approach, adding noise to datasets to protect individual information while still allowing for useful data analysis. These technologies illustrate that it is possible to balance personalization with privacy through creative and thoughtful engineering.

Global Collaboration for Privacy Standards - As data crosses borders, the challenge of balancing personalization and privacy becomes a global issue. International collaboration is crucial for establishing consistent data privacy standards that can be applied worldwide. Organizations like the International Telecommunication

Union (ITU) and the Organisation for Economic Co-operation and Development (OECD) are working to promote global frameworks for data protection. Cross-border data agreements can ensure that privacy rights are respected regardless of where a user lives, creating a more unified approach to data privacy.

In conclusion, balancing personalization with privacy rights is a complex but essential goal in the digital age. By combining transparency, user control, ethical AI practices, robust regulatory frameworks, and technological innovation, we can create a digital environment that respects user privacy while providing the benefits of personalization. It's a multifaceted challenge that requires collaboration among users, companies, governments, and technologists, but it is crucial for building a more ethical and user-friendly digital future.

Summary of Chapter 3

The Personalization-Privacy Paradox is a reflection of the ongoing struggle between the desire for convenient, tailored experiences and the right to privacy in the digital world. While personalization offers undeniable benefits, such as efficiency and relevance, it comes at the cost of extensive data collection and potential misuse. Understanding the data economy and the mechanics of user consent is critical for navigating this landscape. By exploring strategies like transparency, user control, ethical AI, and privacy-enhancing technologies, we can strive to balance these competing interests. The road ahead requires a collective commitment to ethical data practices and robust regulations that protect users without stifling innovation.

Chapter 4. AI in the Workplace: Automation and Beyond

The integration of artificial intelligence (AI) into the workplace is fundamentally changing the nature of work, with both exciting possibilities and significant challenges. AI is automating routine tasks, augmenting human skills to improve productivity and efficiency, and introducing new forms of workplace surveillance. This chapter explores these transformations in detail, examining the trends and implications of AI automation, the ways AI can enhance human capabilities, and the ethical dilemmas associated with monitoring employees.

Automation Trends and Job Displacement

AI-driven automation is transforming industries at an unprecedented pace, and it has sparked a mix of optimism and anxiety about the future of work. Automation refers to the use of machines and software to perform tasks that were traditionally done by humans. The aim is to increase efficiency, reduce human error, and lower operational costs. In the manufacturing sector, robots on assembly lines have replaced manual labor, handling tasks like welding, painting, and packaging with incredible speed and precision. Self-driving vehicles are being tested for logistics and delivery, with the potential to revolutionize transportation.

In the service industry, AI-powered chatbots handle customer service inquiries around the clock, providing immediate assistance and reducing the need for human agents. In finance, algorithms analyze vast amounts of data to make trading decisions, detect fraudulent activity, and automate bookkeeping. Even in healthcare, AI systems assist in scheduling appointments, processing insurance claims, and analyzing patient data.

The Impact on Employment - The widespread adoption of automation has raised concerns about job displacement, as machines and AI systems take over roles that were once the domain of human workers. This impact is most visible in sectors like manufacturing and retail, where repetitive tasks are highly susceptible to automation. Cashiers, factory workers, and data entry clerks are among those whose jobs are at high risk of being automated. The fear of job loss extends to more specialized roles, as AI becomes increasingly capable of performing cognitive tasks, such as legal research, medical diagnosis, and even financial analysis.

However, history has shown that while technology can eliminate certain jobs, it often creates new ones. The rise of AI has led to a demand for professionals skilled in programming, data analysis, machine learning, and AI maintenance. New roles are also emerging, such as AI ethicists, who ensure that AI systems operate in a fair and transparent manner, and data privacy officers, who manage the security of sensitive information. Additionally, automation can free employees from monotonous tasks, allowing them to focus on more creative, strategic, or human-centric work.

The challenge lies in the transition. Workers whose jobs are automated may struggle to adapt if they do not have the skills needed for the new roles created by AI. This highlights the importance of retraining and reskilling programs, which governments and businesses must prioritize to ensure a smooth transition into the AI-driven workforce. Education systems may also need to evolve, emphasizing critical thinking, adaptability, and digital literacy.

Broader Societal Implications - The impact of automation extends beyond individual workers to the broader economy. While increased productivity can lead to economic growth, the benefits are not always evenly distributed. There is a risk of widening income inequality, as highly skilled workers who can adapt to the new technology thrive, while low-skilled workers are left behind. Policymakers must consider how to mitigate these effects, perhaps through social safety nets, universal basic income, or incentives for companies to invest in human capital.

Augmenting Human Skills with AI

While automation often raises fears of job loss, AI also has the potential to augment human abilities rather than replace them. AI augmentation refers to the use of technology to enhance human performance, making people more effective in their roles. Instead of viewing AI as a threat, many experts see it as a tool that can work alongside humans to improve outcomes, streamline processes, and spark innovation.

AI in Healthcare - In the healthcare sector, AI is making a significant impact by assisting doctors, nurses, and researchers. For example, AI-driven diagnostic tools can analyze medical images—such as X-rays, MRIs, and CT scans—with remarkable accuracy. These systems can detect signs of diseases like cancer or fractures that might be missed by the human eye. By identifying patterns in medical data, AI can help doctors make quicker and more accurate diagnoses. However, the human element remains crucial: while AI can highlight potential issues, doctors use their clinical expertise to interpret the results and decide on treatment plans. This partnership allows for better patient outcomes and more efficient use of healthcare resources.

AI is also being used to personalize medicine. Machine learning models analyze genetic data, lifestyle factors, and medical history to recommend treatments tailored to individual patients. This approach holds promise for improving the effectiveness of treatments and reducing side effects. In medical research, AI accelerates the process of drug discovery by analyzing vast datasets and identifying promising compounds, cutting years off the traditional development timeline.

AI in Business and Data Analysis - In the corporate world, AI-powered analytics tools are revolutionizing how businesses make decisions. These tools can process massive datasets in seconds, uncovering trends and insights that would take human analysts weeks to find. For example, AI can analyze consumer behavior to help companies tailor their marketing strategies or optimize supply chains to reduce waste and lower costs. Executives can use these insights to make data-driven decisions that boost efficiency and profitability.

AI is also transforming human resources (HR) departments. AI algorithms can scan resumes to shortlist candidates who are the best fit for a job, analyze employee performance data to identify areas for improvement, and even predict which employees are at risk of leaving the company. While these applications increase efficiency, they also raise questions about fairness and transparency, which we will explore later in this chapter.

Creative and Educational Applications - AI is proving to be a valuable tool in creative industries as well. Graphic designers use AI to generate design concepts, automate image editing, and create animations, speeding up the creative process. Writers can use AI for inspiration, grammar checking, and even content generation. Musicians are experimenting with AI to compose music, blending human creativity with machine-generated melodies. In these fields, AI acts as a collaborator, enhancing human creativity rather than replacing it.

In education, AI-powered platforms personalize learning experiences for students. These systems assess each student's strengths and weaknesses and adapt lessons to their individual needs. For teachers, AI can automate grading and administrative tasks, freeing up more time for one-on-one instruction and lesson planning. In corporate settings, AI-driven training programs help employees learn new skills more efficiently, which is essential in today's rapidly changing work environment.

The future of work will likely involve even closer collaboration between humans and machines. To make the most of AI augmentation, organizations must invest in training and change management. Employees need to understand how to use AI tools effectively, and companies must foster a culture that embraces innovation while being mindful of the ethical implications.

The Ethics of Workplace Surveillance

The integration of AI into workplace monitoring has sparked a heated debate about privacy, trust, and the balance between productivity and employee rights. AI-powered surveillance tools are used by many companies to monitor employee behavior, analyze productivity metrics, and ensure compliance with company policies. While these technologies offer undeniable benefits, they also present ethical and moral dilemmas that need to be carefully addressed.

How AI Surveillance Works - AI surveillance tools can range from simple software that tracks computer usage to complex systems that monitor physical movements in a warehouse or analyze employee communications. For example, in a corporate office, AI software might track how much time employees spend on different tasks, monitor their email and chat communications for signs of inappropriate behavior, or analyze productivity patterns to recommend workflow optimizations. In warehouses or factories, AI systems use sensors and cameras to monitor worker movements, ensuring safety and efficiency.

In the age of remote work, AI surveillance has taken on new forms. Companies use software that tracks keystrokes, takes periodic screenshots, or even uses webcams to ensure employees are actively working. Some systems analyze employees' facial expressions during video calls to gauge engagement or detect signs of stress.

Privacy and Trust Issues - The use of AI for workplace surveillance raises serious concerns about privacy and trust. Employees may feel that their every move is being scrutinized, which can lead to anxiety and decreased job satisfaction. The feeling of being constantly monitored can create a toxic work environment, where employees are afraid to take breaks or engage in casual conversations. Additionally, there is a risk of misuse or abuse of surveillance data. For instance, if an AI system flags an employee as underperforming based on its metrics, should that employee be penalized without considering the context or human judgment?

Another concern is data security. The more data a company collects about its employees, the greater the risk of that information being leaked or hacked. Sensitive data, such as private conversations or health information, could be exposed, leading to significant consequences for individuals. There is also the issue of algorithmic bias. If an AI surveillance system is trained on biased data, it may unfairly target certain employees or make inaccurate assessments.

Finding a Balance - To balance the benefits of AI surveillance with the rights of employees, companies must adopt transparent and ethical practices. Employees should be informed about what data is being collected, how it will be used, and who will have access to it. Consent should be sought wherever possible, and employees should have a clear understanding of the surveillance measures in place. This transparency is essential to building trust between employers and employees and ensuring that surveillance tools are used fairly and responsibly.

Companies should also consider implementing measures that limit the invasiveness of AI monitoring. For example, surveillance could be limited to work-related activities, and data collection should be minimized to only what is necessary for ensuring productivity and safety. In cases where AI monitoring is used for performance evaluations, human oversight should always be involved to account for context and provide a more holistic assessment. Employers must also ensure that data collected is stored securely and used ethically, with strict protocols to prevent misuse or unauthorized access.

Ethical Frameworks and Regulations - Governments and regulatory bodies are beginning to address the ethical concerns surrounding workplace surveillance. In some regions, laws are being introduced to protect employee privacy and limit the extent to which companies can monitor their staff. For example, the European Union's

General Data Protection Regulation (GDPR) provides guidelines on data privacy and requires companies to justify their use of surveillance technologies. These regulations help ensure that employee rights are not violated in the pursuit of increased productivity.

However, regulations alone may not be enough. Companies must also establish internal ethical guidelines for AI surveillance. This includes conducting regular audits to identify potential biases in surveillance systems, ensuring that monitoring practices are equitable, and creating channels for employees to voice their concerns. The role of AI ethics committees in organizations is becoming increasingly important, as these groups can provide oversight and ensure that technology is being used in a way that aligns with the company's values.

The ethics of workplace surveillance ultimately come down to a balance between organizational needs and employee well-being. While AI has the potential to improve efficiency and safety, it must be deployed in a way that respects human dignity and fosters a positive work environment.

Summary of Chapter 4

AI has profoundly impacted the workplace, driving automation, enhancing human skills, and introducing new surveillance technologies. Automation trends are reshaping entire industries, raising concerns about job displacement but also creating opportunities for new roles and career paths. AI augmentation demonstrates the potential for collaboration between humans and machines, enabling greater efficiency and innovation across various fields, from healthcare to education. However, the ethical challenges of AI-driven workplace surveillance cannot be ignored. Organizations must find a way to balance the benefits of monitoring with respect for employee privacy and autonomy. As we continue to integrate AI into the world of work, ethical considerations must remain a top priority, and ongoing dialogue among all stakeholders will be essential to create fair and productive work environments.

Chapter 5. Education Revolution: AI-Powered Learning

The integration of artificial intelligence (AI) into education is transforming traditional learning methods, paving the way for a more personalized, efficient, and data-driven educational experience. This chapter explores the profound impact of AI in learning environments, focusing on adaptive learning systems, AI's role in curriculum development, and the significant challenges and limitations that come with implementing these technologies. As AI continues to reshape education, understanding both its benefits and drawbacks is essential for creating a balanced and effective learning ecosystem.

Adaptive Learning Systems

Adaptive learning systems have revolutionized education by offering a personalized learning experience tailored to each student's needs. These systems leverage AI algorithms to analyze data from students' interactions and adjust the learning material accordingly. Instead of a standardized approach where all students' progress at the same pace, adaptive learning ensures that each learner can advance through the curriculum based on their unique abilities and comprehension levels.

How Adaptive Learning Systems Work - At the heart of adaptive learning systems is the ability to continuously assess a student's performance. The system collects data on how well a student understands each concept and identifies patterns in their learning behavior. If a student struggles with a particular topic, the system may provide additional resources, such as explanatory videos, interactive exercises, or simpler explanations to help them grasp the material. On the other hand, if a student shows mastery of a concept, the system will introduce more challenging material to keep them engaged and intellectually stimulated.

Imagine a high school math class using an adaptive learning platform. One student may need extra help with algebraic equations, so the system offers targeted practice problems and step-by-step guides. Another student who excels in the same topic can be directed to more advanced problems or real-world applications of algebra. This personalized approach allows students to learn at their own pace, fostering a deeper understanding of the material and reducing the frustration that often comes with rigid, one-size-fits-all education.

Teachers also benefit from adaptive learning systems. These platforms generate detailed reports on each student's progress, highlighting areas where they are excelling or struggling. With this data, teachers can make informed decisions about their instructional strategies, providing additional support where needed or celebrating achievements. Adaptive learning systems can also identify class-wide trends, helping educators understand which topics may require a different teaching approach.

Benefits and Drawbacks of Adaptive Learning - The benefits of adaptive learning are significant. By personalizing education, these systems keep students engaged and motivated. They also reduce the achievement gap by providing struggling learners with the resources they need to catch up. Additionally, adaptive learning saves time for both students and teachers, as it eliminates the need to spend equal time on topics that some students may already understand.

However, adaptive learning is not without challenges. One major concern is the risk of over-reliance on technology. While AI systems can offer personalized content, they cannot replace the human touch that is vital for social and emotional learning. Teachers provide mentorship, motivation, and a sense of community—elements that technology alone cannot replicate. Furthermore, there is the issue of accessibility. Not all students have equal access to adaptive learning technology, especially in underfunded schools or remote areas, which can exacerbate educational inequalities.

AI in Curriculum Development

AI is also transforming curriculum development, making it more efficient, dynamic, and data-driven. Traditional curriculum design is a time-consuming process that requires meticulous planning and constant updates to remain relevant. AI is streamlining this process by analyzing vast amounts of data to identify gaps in the curriculum, suggest new topics, and optimize lesson plans for better learning outcomes.

The Role of AI in Curriculum Design - AI-powered tools can analyze student performance data, test results, and feedback to provide insights into the effectiveness of existing curricula. For example, if students across different schools consistently struggle with a particular math concept, an AI system can flag this issue and recommend additional instructional materials or an alternative teaching method. Conversely, if a certain teaching approach yields excellent results, AI can suggest incorporating similar strategies in other parts of the curriculum.

One of the key advantages of using AI in curriculum development is its ability to personalize learning materials. In language learning, for instance, AI can adjust vocabulary lessons based on a student's current proficiency level and areas of interest. If a student is passionate about sports, the AI system might include sports-related vocabulary in language exercises, making learning more engaging and relevant. Additionally, AI tools can create a variety of assessment formats, from multiple-choice questions to open-ended essays, to evaluate student understanding comprehensively.

AI also aids in updating and refining curricula to reflect the latest advancements in various fields. In subjects like science and technology, where knowledge is constantly evolving, AI can help educators stay up-to-date by suggesting new topics and resources. For teachers, this means less time spent on administrative tasks and more time focused on engaging with students.

Benefits for Educators and Students - For educators, AI-driven curriculum development tools simplify the planning process and provide actionable insights that can enhance teaching effectiveness. These systems allow teachers to tailor their lesson plans to the unique needs of their students, fostering a more inclusive and engaging classroom environment. For students, an AI-enhanced curriculum ensures that learning materials are relevant, up-to-date, and presented in a way that suits their individual learning styles.

However, the use of AI in curriculum development also raises concerns. One of the biggest challenges is maintaining academic freedom and creativity. Some educator's worry that AI-generated curricula may limit their ability to bring their own ideas and teaching styles into the classroom. There is also the question of data privacy, as AI systems require access to sensitive information about students. Ensuring the security of this data and complying with privacy regulations is crucial.

Challenges and Limitations in AI Education

Despite the promise of AI in revolutionizing education, there are significant challenges and limitations that must be addressed. These challenges include issues of accessibility, the potential for bias in AI systems, the irreplaceable value of human interaction in education, and concerns about data privacy and security.

Accessibility and the Digital Divide - One of the most pressing challenges is the digital divide, which refers to the gap between those who have access to technology and those who do not. While well-funded schools in urban areas may have the resources to implement AI-powered learning tools, many schools in rural or low-income areas lack the necessary infrastructure. This disparity creates an unequal educational experience, where some students benefit from cutting-edge technology while others are left behind. Bridging this gap requires significant investment in technology infrastructure, teacher training, and equitable resource distribution.

Bias and Quality Concerns in AI Systems - Another critical issue is the potential for bias in AI algorithms. AI systems are trained on data, and if that data contains biases, the system can perpetuate or even exacerbate those biases. For example, an AI tool used to grade essays might favor writing styles or cultural references that align with the training data, disadvantaging students from different backgrounds. This is especially concerning when AI is used for assessments, college admissions, or any process that impacts a student's future opportunities. Developers must prioritize fairness and conduct regular audits to ensure that AI systems are unbiased and equitable.

The quality and reliability of AI systems also come into question. While AI can provide valuable insights, it is not infallible. Mistakes in data analysis or algorithmic errors can lead to incorrect assessments, misaligned curricula, or even harm to students' learning outcomes. Educators must be trained to recognize and address these limitations, using AI as a tool rather than a replacement for human judgment.

The Human Element in Education - AI can enhance education, but it cannot replace the human element that is crucial for holistic learning. Teachers do more than deliver content; they inspire, mentor, and support students emotionally and socially. The ability to understand a student's unique challenges, motivate them, and foster critical thinking skills is something that AI cannot replicate. Furthermore, collaborative activities, discussions, and hands-on projects play a significant role in developing social skills and emotional intelligence—areas where human interaction is irreplaceable.

Data Privacy and Security - The use of AI in education raises serious concerns about data privacy and security. AI systems often require access to personal and academic information, including learning habits, assessment results, and behavioral data. Protecting this information from data breaches and unauthorized use is paramount. Schools and educational institutions must implement strict data protection measures, comply with privacy regulations, and be transparent about how data is collected and used. Parents and students also need to be educated about data privacy and their rights in the digital age.

Ensuring ethical and secure use of AI in education requires collaboration among educators, policymakers, developers, and the broader community. It also calls for ongoing dialogue and the development of ethical guidelines to protect students while leveraging the benefits of AI technology.

Summary of Chapter 5

The integration of AI in education is a double-edged sword, offering incredible opportunities for personalized and efficient learning while also presenting complex challenges. Adaptive learning systems have revolutionized how students engage with material, allowing for a customized approach that can address individual needs and keep learners motivated. However, the reliance on AI must be balanced with human interaction to ensure that education remains holistic, addressing emotional, social, and critical thinking aspects.

AI in curriculum development offers educators powerful tools for creating effective and up-to-date lesson plans, but it comes with concerns about academic freedom and data privacy. The potential for AI to introduce or perpetuate biases underscores the need for fairness and rigorous oversight. Accessibility remains a critical issue, as not all students have equal opportunities to benefit from these technologies, potentially widening educational disparities.

Ultimately, the education revolution driven by AI holds immense promise, but it also demands a thoughtful and balanced approach. Educators, policymakers, and technology developers must collaborate to harness the power of AI while safeguarding the values and principles that make education meaningful. As we move forward, the goal should be to create an inclusive, ethical, and effective educational ecosystem where technology enhances, rather than replaces, the human experience.

Chapter 6. Smart Homes: Convenience and Control

The advent of smart home technology has revolutionized the way we live, offering unparalleled convenience, efficiency, and control over our living environments. From voice-activated assistants to AI-driven energy management and home security systems, the modern home is becoming increasingly intelligent. However, the benefits of smart living come with challenges, particularly regarding privacy and data security. This chapter explores the transformative role of AI in home automation, delves into the critical privacy concerns associated with smart homes, and discusses future innovations that could redefine how we live.

The Role of AI in Home Automation

Artificial intelligence is at the core of smart home automation, making everyday tasks more convenient and efficient. AI technology powers a range of smart home devices that learn from user behavior, make autonomous decisions, and communicate with other connected devices. This automation allows homeowners to control almost every aspect of their living environment with minimal effort, enhancing both comfort and functionality.

Smart Assistants and Voice Control - One of the most widespread and user-friendly applications of AI in home automation is the use of smart voice assistants. Devices like Amazon's Alexa, Google Assistant, and Apple's Siri have become household staples, capable of performing a wide variety of tasks through simple voice commands. These voice assistants can set reminders, play music, provide weather updates, and even control other smart devices in the home, such as lights, thermostats, and locks. The integration of these assistants with other smart devices allows for seamless home management. For instance, you can say, "Alexa, I'm leaving," and your home will automatically lock the doors, turn off the lights, and set the thermostat to energy-saving mode.

AI-Driven Energy Management - Energy management is another area where AI has made a substantial impact. Smart thermostats, such as Nest and Ecobee, use machine learning to understand a homeowner's heating and cooling preferences and adjust settings accordingly. These thermostats can detect when a home is empty and shift to energy-saving modes, thereby lowering energy bills and reducing the home's carbon footprint. AI-driven energy management extends to smart lighting systems like Philips Hue, which can be scheduled to turn on or off based on room occupancy or daylight availability. These systems not only enhance convenience but also contribute to a more sustainable lifestyle.

Home Security and Safety - AI has significantly advanced home security through the use of smart cameras, locks, and alarm systems. Smart security cameras equipped with AI can distinguish between familiar faces and strangers, reducing the frequency of false alarms and enhancing overall security. These cameras can send real-time alerts to your smartphone, allowing you to monitor your home even when you're away. AI-powered smart locks provide additional layers of security, enabling homeowners to lock or unlock their doors remotely or through biometric authentication, such as fingerprint scanning or facial recognition.

Home safety has also improved with AI technology. Smart smoke and carbon monoxide detectors, such as those offered by Nest Protect, can send notifications to your phone if an alarm is triggered, ensuring that you are alerted even if you're not home. Additionally, AI-powered leak detectors can identify water leaks in real-time, helping to prevent extensive damage by notifying homeowners or shutting off the water supply automatically.

Entertainment and Convenience - AI enhances home entertainment systems by learning user preferences and delivering customized content. Smart TVs use AI to recommend shows and movies based on viewing habits, while smart speakers can curate playlists that match your mood. Smart refrigerators can keep track of food inventory, suggest recipes based on available ingredients, and even place grocery orders when supplies are running low. The convenience offered by these AI-powered devices makes home life smoother and more enjoyable.

While the role of AI in home automation brings immense benefits, it also raises questions about dependency on technology and the potential risks of malfunctions or system failures. As smart homes become more complex, ensuring the reliability and security of these systems becomes increasingly critical.

Privacy Concerns in Smart Home Environments

The integration of AI technology into our homes brings not only convenience but also significant privacy concerns. Smart home devices collect and process an extensive amount of personal data, raising questions about how this data is used, stored, and protected. Understanding these privacy issues is crucial for anyone using or considering the adoption of smart home technology.

Data Collection and Usage - Smart home devices continuously collect data to function and improve their services. This data includes everything from audio recordings captured by voice assistants to video footage from security cameras and usage patterns from smart appliances. For example, a smart thermostat may track when you are home, your preferred temperature settings, and how often you adjust the thermostat. Voice assistants like Amazon Alexa and Google Assistant record voice commands and may store audio files to enhance voice recognition capabilities. Smart doorbells with cameras record who comes and goes, while smart TVs can collect data on viewing habits and preferences.

The concern is that all this data is often stored in the cloud and managed by the companies that manufacture these devices. While this data collection enables advanced features and personalized experiences, it also poses a risk. Companies may use this data for targeted advertising or share it with third parties, sometimes without explicit user consent. Additionally, the sheer volume of data collected increases the potential for misuse, whether through data breaches or unauthorized access.

Vulnerability to Hacking and Cyberattacks - One of the most alarming privacy concerns in smart home environments is the risk of hacking. Because smart home devices are interconnected and often connected to the internet, they can be vulnerable to cyberattacks. Hackers who gain access to a smart home network could potentially control devices, spy on homeowners, or disable security systems. The consequences of a cyberattack can range from minor annoyances, like adjusting the thermostat, to severe security threats, such as unlocking doors or accessing live camera feeds.

Moreover, some smart home devices have been reported to have weak security features, such as default passwords that users never change. This makes them easy targets for hackers. The interconnected nature of these devices means that compromising one device could give a hacker access to the entire network, making comprehensive cybersecurity measures essential.

Concerns about Surveillance and Data Misuse - Many smart home devices come with built-in cameras and microphones, raising concerns about surveillance. There have been instances where voice assistants have accidentally recorded private conversations and, in some cases, sent them to unintended recipients. Similarly, smart TVs and baby monitors have had vulnerabilities that allowed unauthorized users to access video or audio feeds. The idea that a device in your home could be listening or watching without your knowledge is unsettling, and it challenges traditional notions of privacy.

Even when companies claim that data is used only to improve services, the potential for misuse remains. For example, data collected by smart home devices could be subpoenaed in legal cases or used for surveillance by law enforcement. In some cases, companies have faced backlash for using data in ways that were not transparent or for failing to protect user privacy adequately.

How to Protect Your Privacy - To mitigate privacy risks, smart home users must be proactive. One of the simplest yet most effective measures is to use strong, unique passwords for each device and to enable two-factor authentication whenever possible. Regularly updating device software is crucial, as updates often include security patches to fix vulnerabilities. Disabling features that are not in use, such as always-on microphones or cameras, can also reduce risk.

It is also important to read the privacy policies of smart home devices and understand what data is being collected and how it will be used. Choosing devices from reputable companies that prioritize data security and offer end-to-end encryption is another way to enhance privacy. Being informed and cautious can go a long way in protecting your personal data in a smart home environment.

Future Innovations in Smart Living

The future of smart homes is incredibly promising, with innovations that will make living environments even more intelligent, sustainable, and responsive to human needs. As AI and IoT technologies continue to evolve, we can expect a new wave of advancements that will redefine what it means to live in a connected home.

AI-Powered Predictive Maintenance - One of the most anticipated future innovations in smart living is AI-powered predictive maintenance. In the future, smart home systems will be able to monitor appliances and home infrastructure in real-time, predicting when maintenance is needed. For instance, a smart washing machine could analyze its performance data and notify homeowners when a part is likely to wear out. Similarly, smart HVAC systems could detect inefficiencies and suggest maintenance before a breakdown occurs. This not only extends the lifespan of home appliances but also saves homeowners money on repairs and reduces the inconvenience of unexpected failures.

Advanced Health and Wellness Monitoring - AI technology is set to play a significant role in health and wellness monitoring within smart homes. Future systems will be capable of tracking vital signs, monitoring sleep patterns, and even detecting changes in behavior that could indicate health issues. For example, a smart bathroom mirror could analyze your skin condition and detect early signs of dehydration or stress. AI-powered health monitoring could also be invaluable for elderly residents or those with chronic illnesses. Sensors embedded throughout the home could detect falls, track medication adherence, and alert family members or healthcare providers in case of an emergency.

Sustainability and Energy Optimization - As concerns about climate change grow, future smart homes will be designed with sustainability in mind. AI will be used to optimize energy consumption through advanced energy management systems. These systems will coordinate all energy-consuming devices in the home to minimize waste and maximize efficiency. For example, AI could analyze weather forecasts and adjust solar panel usage, energy storage, and heating or cooling schedules to ensure optimal energy performance. Smart grids will enable homes to buy and sell energy dynamically, sharing excess power generated by solar panels with the community or drawing energy during non-peak hours to reduce costs.

Smart water management systems will also become more advanced. These systems will use AI to monitor water usage, detect leaks in real-time, and suggest ways to reduce water waste. For example, a smart irrigation system could adjust watering schedules based on soil moisture levels and local weather forecasts, ensuring that gardens are only watered when necessary. These innovations will not only save resources but also contribute to a more sustainable and eco-friendly lifestyle.

Integration with Smart Cities - The future of smart homes will be closely linked to the development of smart cities. As urban areas become more connected, smart homes will be able to interact with city infrastructure to improve the quality of life for residents. For example, smart traffic management systems could communicate with smart home devices to optimize travel routes and reduce congestion. Waste management could be made more efficient, with smart homes notifying residents when garbage collection is scheduled or integrating with city services to optimize waste disposal.

Another exciting possibility is the integration of emergency response systems. In the event of a natural disaster, smart homes could receive alerts from city systems and automatically take protective measures, such as closing storm shutters or shutting off gas lines. Homes could also provide real-time data to emergency responders, helping them better understand and manage crises.

Immersive and Personalized Experiences - As AI technology advances, smart homes will become even more personalized and immersive. Virtual reality (VR) and augmented reality (AR) will be integrated into everyday home activities, from immersive home offices to virtual fitness programs. Imagine a home gym where AR technology creates a virtual environment for your workout, or a home office setup that uses VR to make remote work feel more engaging and interactive.

AI will also continue to refine home entertainment. Smart speakers and home theater systems will become even more intuitive, adapting to your preferences and creating fully immersive experiences. Lighting, sound, and even ambient temperature could adjust dynamically to enhance your movie nights, dinner parties, or meditation sessions. AI will curate experiences based on your routines and habits, offering everything from personalized morning routines to curated music playlists that evolve throughout the day.

Future Challenges and Ethical Considerations - While these future innovations are exciting, they also come with challenges. The more interconnected our homes become, the more data they generate, and this raises questions about data security, ethical use of AI, and the potential for surveillance. There will need to be robust regulations and guidelines to ensure that the technology is used responsibly and ethically. Additionally, making these advanced technologies accessible to all socioeconomic groups will be crucial to prevent further inequality in the digital age.

Summary of Chapter 6

Smart homes, powered by AI, are redefining how we interact with our living environments. From voice-activated assistants to intelligent energy management systems and advanced home security, AI makes our lives more convenient, efficient, and secure. However, this convenience comes with privacy concerns, as smart home devices collect vast amounts of personal data and are vulnerable to hacking. Future innovations promise even more advancements, including predictive maintenance, health monitoring, and integration with smart city infrastructure, but they also require careful consideration of ethical and security implications. As we move toward a more connected future, balancing convenience with control and privacy will be key to enjoying the benefits of smart living responsibly.

Chapter 7. The Rise of Smart Cities and Urban AI

The concept of smart cities, powered by artificial intelligence (AI) and data analytics, is revolutionizing urban living. As urban populations grow and challenges like congestion, pollution, and resource management become more pressing, cities are leveraging technology to improve infrastructure, optimize public services, and make urban spaces more efficient and sustainable. However, the rise of smart cities also brings significant ethical and privacy concerns that must be carefully addressed. This chapter delves into how AI is transforming urban infrastructure, how data is enhancing public services, and the ethical considerations that come with integrating AI into city management.

Infrastructure Powered by AI

Urban infrastructure is being transformed through the use of AI, making cities more efficient, responsive, and environmentally friendly. From traffic management systems that minimize congestion to smart grids that optimize energy use, AI is redefining how cities function. The implementation of AI in infrastructure is not just about automation; it's about creating a self-sustaining ecosystem that improves the quality of life for residents.

AI in Traffic and Transportation Management

Traffic congestion is one of the biggest challenges faced by urban areas, leading to lost productivity, increased emissions, and higher stress levels for commuters. AI-driven traffic management systems are now being deployed to tackle this issue. These systems collect real-time data from sources like traffic cameras, GPS devices, and sensors embedded in roads. AI algorithms analyze this data to detect patterns and predict traffic flow, adjusting traffic signals dynamically to reduce congestion. For example, during peak hours, AI can optimize the timing of traffic lights to allow a smoother flow of vehicles, reducing gridlock and travel time.

Public transportation is also being revolutionized by AI. Buses, trains, and subways are becoming more efficient as AI systems analyze passenger data and adjust schedules accordingly. Predictive maintenance powered by AI helps ensure that public transit vehicles are in good working order, minimizing delays and breakdowns. Autonomous vehicles, which are currently being tested in many cities, have the potential to transform public transportation by providing safer and more reliable options for getting around. Self-driving buses and shuttles could soon be a regular feature in smart cities, reducing human error and making transportation more accessible to everyone, including the elderly and disabled.

Smart Energy Grids and Sustainable Infrastructure - Another significant application of AI in urban infrastructure is in energy management through smart grids. Traditional energy grids are often inefficient, but smart grids use AI to monitor and distribute electricity more effectively. AI can predict energy demand based on factors like weather conditions and historical data, allowing for a more balanced energy supply. During high-demand periods, AI can prioritize energy distribution to critical services, such as hospitals, while encouraging less essential services to reduce consumption.

Smart buildings are also an integral part of a city's energy efficiency. These buildings use AI and IoT sensors to optimize energy usage, automatically adjusting heating, cooling, and lighting based on occupancy and time of day. For example, if a room is empty, the lights and air conditioning can turn off to conserve energy. In addition to energy management, AI is being used to monitor water consumption, detect leaks, and manage waste. Smart irrigation systems in public parks use AI to water plants only when necessary, saving water and keeping green spaces healthy.

Waste Management and Environmental Monitoring - Effective waste management is crucial for maintaining a clean and sustainable urban environment. AI is revolutionizing how cities handle waste by optimizing collection routes and schedules. Smart waste bins equipped with sensors can notify waste management services when they are full, reducing unnecessary pickups and minimizing fuel consumption. AI can also analyze data to identify waste production trends, enabling cities to implement targeted recycling and waste reduction programs.

Environmental monitoring is another critical area where AI is making a difference. AI systems use data from air quality sensors, weather stations, and satellite imagery to monitor pollution levels in real time. If air quality drops to unsafe levels, city officials can issue alerts and take measures to protect residents, such as restricting vehicle traffic or increasing public transportation options. AI can also be used to predict and mitigate the impact of natural disasters, such as floods and hurricanes, by analyzing environmental data and providing early warnings.

Enhancing Public Services with Data

Smart cities harness the power of data to optimize public services, making them more efficient and responsive to the needs of residents. By collecting and analyzing vast amounts of data, city officials can make evidence-based decisions that improve healthcare, public safety, utilities, and education. Data-driven insights are helping cities provide better services while also being more sustainable and cost-effective.

AI in Healthcare and Emergency Response - AI and data analytics are revolutionizing healthcare in urban areas by making services more proactive and efficient. One of the most promising applications is in disease prevention. AI can analyze health data from hospitals, clinics, pharmacies, and even social media to identify patterns and predict disease outbreaks. For instance, if there is a spike in people buying flu medication or visiting emergency rooms with respiratory symptoms, AI can alert public health officials to a potential outbreak. This allows cities to deploy medical resources quickly and contain the spread of diseases.

Emergency response services are also becoming smarter thanks to AI. AI algorithms analyze historical incident data, traffic patterns, and current conditions to determine the fastest routes for emergency vehicles, minimizing response times. For example, AI can help ambulances navigate through congested areas more efficiently, potentially saving lives. In the future, drones equipped with AI could be used to deliver medical supplies to accident scenes or hard-to-reach areas, providing immediate assistance while waiting for paramedics.

Public Safety and AI Surveillance - AI is being used to enhance public safety through surveillance and predictive policing. AI-powered surveillance cameras equipped with computer vision can detect unusual activities, such as a fight breaking out or a suspicious package being left unattended. These systems can alert authorities in real time, allowing for a quicker response. Predictive policing uses data from crime reports, social media, and public events to identify potential crime hotspots and allocate police resources more effectively. While these technologies have the potential to make cities safer, they also raise concerns about privacy and surveillance, which will be discussed in the next section.

Smart Water Management and Utilities - Efficient management of water and utilities is critical for sustainable urban living. AI-driven water management systems use sensors to monitor water quality and detect leaks in real time. By identifying issues early, these systems can prevent water loss and ensure that residents have access to clean and safe drinking water. In utilities, AI helps optimize energy and water distribution, reducing waste and lowering costs. For example, AI can predict peak usage times and adjust resource allocation to prevent shortages.

Education and Citizen Engagement - Smart cities are also improving education and citizen engagement through data analytics. AI can analyze data on school performance, student attendance, and community needs to allocate educational resources more effectively. For example, if data shows that a certain area has a high dropout rate, city officials can invest in after-school programs or community centers to support students. AI-driven platforms also enable better communication between city governments and residents. Chatbots can provide residents with real-time information about city services, answer questions, and even help report issues, like broken streetlights or potholes.

Data-driven community engagement tools allow residents to participate in urban planning decisions. For example, interactive platforms can collect feedback on proposed projects, like new parks or public transportation routes, giving citizens a voice in how their city evolves. By using data to understand the needs and preferences of residents, city planners can create more inclusive and effective urban environments.

Ethical Considerations in Urban AI

As AI becomes an integral part of urban management, it brings with it a host of ethical concerns. The widespread use of AI in smart cities raises questions about privacy, data security, algorithmic bias, and accountability. Addressing these ethical challenges is crucial to ensure that AI technologies are used responsibly and equitably.

Privacy and Data Security - One of the most pressing ethical issues in smart cities is privacy. AI-powered surveillance systems, such as facial recognition cameras and traffic monitoring systems, collect and process vast amounts of personal data. While these technologies can improve public safety and traffic management, they also create a sense of being constantly watched. The potential for misuse of surveillance data, either by governments or third parties, is a significant concern. There have been instances where surveillance technologies have been used for purposes beyond their original intent, such as monitoring political activists or conducting mass surveillance without public consent.

To mitigate privacy risks, smart cities must implement strong data protection measures. This includes encrypting data, anonymizing personal information, and being transparent about data collection practices. Residents should be informed about what data is collected, how it is used, and who has access to it. Consent and opt-out options should be available whenever possible. Regulations, such as the European Union's General Data Protection Regulation (GDPR), serve as examples of how governments can enforce data privacy standards.

Bias and Fairness in AI Systems - AI systems are trained on data, and if this data contains biases, the AI can perpetuate or even amplify these biases. In a smart city context, biased AI algorithms could lead to unfair outcomes, such as discriminatory policing practices or unequal access to public services. For instance, if a predictive policing algorithm is trained on biased historical data, it may disproportionately target certain communities, reinforcing existing inequalities and perpetuating systemic biases. Similarly, if AI systems used for allocating public resources are trained on incomplete or biased data, they may favor certain neighborhoods over others, exacerbating socioeconomic disparities.

To address these issues, it is essential to ensure that AI algorithms are developed and tested with fairness in mind. This involves using diverse and representative data sets, conducting regular audits to identify and correct biases, and involving ethicists and community stakeholders in the development process. Transparency is also crucial: residents should have the right to know how AI decisions are made and be able to challenge those decisions if they feel they are unfair.

Accountability and Governance - Another critical ethical consideration is accountability. In a smart city, who is responsible when an AI system fails or causes harm? For example, if an AI-powered traffic management system malfunctions and causes an accident, who should be held accountable—the city government, the software developers, or the vendors who supplied the technology? Establishing clear lines of accountability is essential for building trust in AI systems.

Governance frameworks must be put in place to ensure that AI technologies are used ethically and responsibly. This includes creating oversight committees, developing ethical guidelines for AI use, and engaging the public in discussions about how AI should be integrated into urban life. These frameworks should also include mechanisms for addressing grievances and holding parties accountable when AI systems cause harm or violate residents' rights.

Public Involvement and Ethical Decision-Making - Ethical considerations in urban AI are not just about technology; they are also about people. Public involvement in decision-making processes is vital to ensure that AI technologies align with the values and needs of the community. Residents should have opportunities to voice their opinions, participate in public consultations, and be actively involved in shaping the future of their cities. This can be achieved through town hall meetings, online forums, and interactive platforms where residents can provide feedback on proposed AI projects.

Engaging the public in ethical decision-making helps create a sense of ownership and trust in smart city initiatives. It also ensures that the deployment of AI technologies is done transparently and inclusively. By prioritizing ethical considerations and involving residents in the governance process, smart cities can leverage the benefits of AI while minimizing risks and ensuring fairness.

Summary of Chapter 7

The rise of smart cities and the integration of urban AI are reshaping how we live, work, and interact in urban environments. AI-powered infrastructure, from traffic management to energy-efficient buildings and environmental monitoring, is making cities more sustainable and responsive to residents' needs. Data-driven public services are improving healthcare, emergency response, education, and citizen engagement, creating more efficient and livable urban spaces. However, the ethical considerations of privacy, data security, bias, and accountability are significant challenges that must be addressed.

Balancing technological advancement with ethical responsibility requires transparent governance, robust data protection measures, and active public involvement. As smart cities continue to evolve, ensuring that AI serves the public good while respecting individual rights will be crucial for creating inclusive and sustainable urban environments. By prioritizing fairness, accountability, and community engagement, smart cities can truly become places where technology enhances quality of life for all residents.

Chapter 8. Healthcare Transformed: AI's Medical Frontier

The integration of artificial intelligence (AI) into healthcare is transforming the landscape of medicine in ways that were once unimaginable. From enhancing diagnostic accuracy to revolutionizing treatment options and expediting medical research, AI's capabilities are reshaping how healthcare professionals deliver care and how patients experience it. However, these advancements come with challenges, including ethical concerns and questions about data privacy and the role of human judgment in medicine. In this chapter, we will explore the multifaceted impact of AI in healthcare, focusing on its applications in diagnosis and treatment, the role of machine learning in research, and the ethical dilemmas posed by AI-driven healthcare.

AI Applications in Diagnosis and Treatment

AI is dramatically changing the way diseases are diagnosed and treated. Its ability to analyze large datasets quickly and accurately is enabling earlier detection of diseases and more personalized treatment plans. These technological advancements are not only saving lives but also improving the efficiency and precision of healthcare delivery.

AI in Medical Imaging and Diagnosis - Medical imaging is one of the areas where AI has made the most significant impact. Radiologists and other medical professionals rely heavily on imaging technologies like X-rays, MRIs, and CT scans to diagnose diseases. However, interpreting these images is complex and prone to human error. AI algorithms trained on millions of medical images can detect patterns and anomalies with a level of accuracy that often surpasses human capabilities. For example, AI can identify early signs of breast cancer, lung nodules, or brain tumors that might be overlooked by even the most experienced radiologists. By catching diseases earlier, patients have a better chance of successful treatment, and healthcare systems can reduce the burden of advanced-stage illnesses.

AI in medical imaging is not limited to radiology. In ophthalmology, AI tools are used to detect diabetic retinopathy and age-related macular degeneration by analyzing retinal images. Dermatology is another field benefiting from AI, with algorithms that can differentiate between benign and malignant skin lesions. These systems empower doctors to make faster and more accurate diagnoses, particularly in settings where specialized expertise may be lacking. However, while AI can be a powerful assistant, the final judgment still lies with human healthcare providers, who consider the patient's overall health and history.

AI in Personalized Treatment - Personalized or precision medicine is another area where AI is making a significant impact. Traditional medical treatments are often one-size-fits-all, but what works for one patient may not work for another due to genetic and lifestyle differences. AI is helping doctors move toward personalized treatment plans by analyzing genetic data, medical history, and even lifestyle factors to determine the most effective therapies for individual patients. For example, in oncology, AI algorithms can analyze a cancer patient's genetic mutations to suggest targeted therapies that are more likely to work and have fewer side effects. This tailored approach improves patient outcomes and reduces the trial-and-error nature of traditional treatments.

Pharmacogenomics, the study of how genes affect a person's response to drugs, is being revolutionized by AI. Machine learning models can predict how a patient will metabolize a specific medication, helping doctors choose the right drug and dosage from the start. This reduces the risk of adverse drug reactions, which are a major cause of hospitalizations. Furthermore, AI-powered wearable devices, like smartwatches and health monitors, continuously track vital signs and alert patients and doctors to potential health problems, such as heart arrhythmias or fluctuations in blood glucose levels. These real-time insights can lead to early interventions and better long-term health management.

Despite the benefits, it is crucial to understand that AI in treatment planning should be used as a tool to augment, not replace, human expertise. Physicians bring empathy, ethical judgment, and a holistic understanding of patient care that AI cannot replicate. Therefore, the best outcomes are often achieved when AI and human clinicians work together, combining the strengths of both.

The Role of Machine Learning in Research

Machine learning, a subset of AI, is transforming the field of medical research. Its ability to analyze massive amounts of data, identify patterns, and generate predictive models is accelerating the pace of scientific discovery. This section explores how machine learning is used in drug discovery, clinical trials, and the understanding of complex diseases.

Accelerating Drug Discovery and Development - The development of new drugs is a long, expensive, and highly uncertain process. On average, it takes over a decade and billions of dollars to bring a new medication to market. Machine learning is revolutionizing this process by making it faster, more cost-effective, and more efficient. AI algorithms can analyze huge datasets of biological, chemical, and medical information to identify potential drug candidates. These algorithms can predict which compounds are likely to interact effectively with disease targets and which are less likely to succeed, significantly reducing the time spent on trial-and-error testing.

One notable example of AI in drug discovery is its use in screening thousands of chemical compounds to find those with the highest probability of treating a specific disease. Machine learning models can simulate how these compounds will interact with human cells, identifying possible side effects or toxicities before any physical testing takes place. This predictive modeling allows researchers to focus their efforts on the most promising candidates, accelerating the development of new therapies for diseases like cancer, Alzheimer's, and infectious diseases.

AI is also being used to repurpose existing drugs for new medical conditions. By analyzing genetic and molecular data, machine learning algorithms can suggest drugs that are already approved for other conditions but may be effective in treating new diseases. This approach has the potential to bring treatments to patients faster, as these drugs have already undergone safety testing.

Improving Clinical Trials - Clinical trials are a critical phase in drug development, but they are often inefficient and costly. Machine learning is improving the design and execution of clinical trials by analyzing patient data to identify the most suitable participants. This ensures that trials have diverse and representative populations, increasing the likelihood of meaningful results. AI algorithms can also predict which patients are more likely to respond to a treatment or experience side effects, making trials more efficient and targeted.

Real-time monitoring of clinical trial participants is another significant advancement enabled by AI. Wearable devices and remote monitoring tools can collect data continuously, providing researchers with up-to-the-minute information on patient health. Machine learning models analyze this data to identify trends and make adjustments to the trial as needed. For example, if a treatment shows early signs of effectiveness or adverse effects, researchers can modify the trial design or halt it altogether, saving time and resources. By making trials more adaptive and data-driven, AI is helping to bring new treatments to market faster.

Understanding and Treating Complex Diseases - Machine learning is also advancing our understanding of complex diseases that have long puzzled scientists. Conditions like cancer, diabetes, and neurodegenerative diseases such as Alzheimer's are influenced by a combination of genetic, environmental, and lifestyle factors. AI can analyze these multifactorial datasets to identify previously unknown risk factors and patterns. For instance, by examining genetic information, lifestyle data, and environmental exposures, AI can predict which individuals are at higher risk for developing certain diseases and suggest preventive measures.

AI is also being used to map the genetic and molecular landscape of diseases, leading to more targeted therapies. For example, in cancer research, AI algorithms analyze tumor samples to identify genetic mutations that drive cancer growth. This information is used to develop precision therapies that target those specific mutations, improving treatment outcomes. Additionally, AI is being used to study the brain's neural networks, providing insights into conditions like Parkinson's and epilepsy and paving the way for new treatment strategies.

Ethical Dilemmas in AI-Driven Healthcare

The use of AI in healthcare raises numerous ethical dilemmas that must be addressed to ensure that these technologies are used responsibly and equitably. Issues such as data privacy, algorithmic bias, the transparency of AI decision-making, and the potential dehumanization of patient care are at the forefront of these concerns.

Data Privacy and Security - AI systems rely on vast amounts of patient data to learn and improve their performance. This data often includes sensitive information such as genetic profiles, medical histories, and real-time health metrics. While the use of this data can lead to life-saving innovations, it also poses significant privacy and security risks. If patient data is not adequately protected, it could be accessed by unauthorized parties, potentially leading to breaches of confidentiality or even identity theft. Additionally, the question of who owns and controls medical data is a contentious issue. Should patients have the right to decide how their data is used, or does the greater good of advancing medical science take precedence?

To address these concerns, healthcare organizations and AI developers must implement robust data security measures, including encryption, secure data storage, and compliance with privacy regulations like the Health Insurance Portability and Accountability Act (HIPAA) in the United States or the General Data Protection Regulation (GDPR) in Europe. Transparent policies about data usage and obtaining informed consent from patients are also essential.

Algorithmic Bias and Fairness - Another major ethical issue is the potential for algorithmic bias. AI systems are only as good as the data they are trained on, and if that data reflects societal biases, the AI can produce biased or unfair outcomes. For example, if an AI model is trained on data that predominantly includes certain demographic groups, it may not perform as well for patients who fall outside of those groups. This can lead to disparities in healthcare, where certain populations receive less accurate diagnoses or less effective treatment recommendations. For instance, an AI system used to detect skin cancer may be trained primarily on images of lighter skin tones, making it less accurate for diagnosing skin conditions in people with darker skin.

Addressing algorithmic bias is critical to ensure equitable healthcare outcomes. This requires using diverse and representative datasets when training AI models, as well as ongoing audits to identify and correct biases. Healthcare organizations should work with ethicists, data scientists, and patient advocacy groups to create systems that are fair and unbiased. Moreover, transparency in AI algorithms is essential. Patients and healthcare providers should understand how AI systems make decisions, especially when those decisions have significant health implications.

Transparency and Explainability - AI in healthcare often operates as a "black box," meaning that even the developers may not fully understand how an AI system arrives at its conclusions. This lack of transparency can be problematic, especially in life-and-death situations. For example, if an AI algorithm recommends a specific treatment plan, doctors and patients need to understand the rationale behind that recommendation. Without explainability, it becomes difficult to trust AI systems or to make informed decisions about patient care.

Efforts are being made to develop explainable AI (XAI) systems that provide clear and understandable explanations of their reasoning. This can help doctors make better use of AI tools and increase patient trust. However, striking the right balance between the complexity of AI models and the need for transparency remains a challenge. In high-stakes healthcare environments, it is crucial for AI systems to be not only accurate but also interpretable.

The Dehumanization of Patient Care - While AI has the potential to greatly improve healthcare, there is a concern that its widespread adoption could lead to the dehumanization of patient care. The doctor-patient relationship is built on trust, empathy, and personalized communication—elements that AI cannot replicate. If healthcare providers rely too heavily on AI, there is a risk that patients may feel treated as data points rather than individuals with unique needs and concerns? The human touch in medicine is irreplaceable, and AI should be used to enhance, not replace, the compassionate care provided by healthcare professionals.

To mitigate this risk, healthcare organizations must ensure that AI tools are used as supplements to human expertise rather than as replacements. Training for healthcare professionals should emphasize the importance of maintaining empathy and a human-centered approach, even as they integrate AI into their practice. Patients should always have the opportunity to discuss AI-generated recommendations with their doctors and have a say in their treatment plans.

Accountability and Liability - Another ethical dilemma is the question of accountability. If an AI system makes a mistake that harms a patient—such as a misdiagnosis or a harmful treatment recommendation—who is responsible? Is it the hospital that implemented the AI, the developers who created the algorithm, or the healthcare provider who relied on the AI's recommendation? Establishing clear lines of accountability is crucial to prevent legal and ethical ambiguity.

Healthcare organizations should have protocols in place for overseeing the use of AI and ensuring that there is always human oversight. Additionally, regulatory bodies may need to update existing laws or create new ones to address the complexities of AI liability in healthcare. Clear guidelines and regulations will help protect both patients and healthcare providers, fostering trust in AI-driven medical technologies.

Summary of Chapter 8

AI is transforming healthcare in profound ways, from enhancing the accuracy of medical diagnoses to accelerating drug discovery and personalizing treatment plans. The use of machine learning in research is unlocking new possibilities for understanding and treating complex diseases, while AI-powered tools are making healthcare more efficient and accessible. However, these advancements come with ethical challenges that must be addressed to ensure that AI serves all patients fairly and equitably. Data privacy, algorithmic bias, the need for transparency, and the potential dehumanization of care are key concerns that require careful oversight and thoughtful solutions.

As AI continues to advance, the collaboration between technology developers, healthcare professionals, policymakers, and ethicists will be essential. By embracing AI responsibly and ethically, we can harness its potential to improve healthcare outcomes while preserving the values of empathy, fairness, and trust that are fundamental to medicine.

Chapter 9. Social Interactions in the Age of Algorithms

Artificial intelligence (AI) has become a central force in shaping our social interactions, especially through social media platforms. Algorithms driven by AI influence what content we see, who we connect with, and even how we feel about ourselves and the world. While these technologies make social media engaging and personalized, they also come with significant psychological and societal impacts. This chapter delves into how AI affects social media dynamics, explores the psychological consequences of algorithmic content feeds, and discusses the critical issue of how algorithms contribute to the spread of both information and misinformation.

AI's Influence on Social Media Dynamics

Social media platforms have evolved into complex ecosystems where content is curated and presented based on AI-driven algorithms. These algorithms are designed to optimize user engagement by showing content that is most likely to hold our attention, keep us engaged, and encourage us to spend more time on the platform. The influence of these algorithms extends beyond what we see; it shapes how we interact with content and with each other.

Content Personalization and Echo Chambers - AI algorithms analyze vast amounts of user data, such as our search history, the posts we like, the people we follow, the videos we watch, and the topics we engage with. Based on this data, the algorithms generate a highly personalized feed that caters to our preferences and interests. For example, if you frequently engage with fitness content, your social media feed will be filled with workout tips, healthy recipes, and gym motivation videos. While this personalization makes the social media experience more relevant and enjoyable, it has significant downsides.

One major drawback is the creation of "echo chambers." An echo chamber occurs when people are exposed only to information and opinions that reinforce their existing beliefs and values. Because the algorithm prioritizes content that aligns with our interests, we end up seeing a narrow, filtered view of the world. This can limit our exposure to diverse viewpoints and contribute to polarization. For instance, in the realm of politics, people who lean toward one side of the political spectrum may only see news and opinions that support their perspective, making it difficult to have balanced and informed discussions.

Engagement-Driven Design and Its Consequences - Social media algorithms are optimized to maximize user engagement. Engagement can include actions like liking a post, sharing a video, commenting on a picture, or even simply spending time scrolling through the feed. To achieve this, AI systems are programmed to prioritize content that evokes strong emotional responses, such as anger, joy, surprise, or outrage. Studies have shown that emotionally charged content is more likely to be shared, which is why controversial or sensational posts often receive more visibility. This creates a cycle where highly engaging content is rewarded, and more nuanced or balanced content is sidelined.

The engagement-driven design of social media platforms can lead to addictive behavior. The algorithms are designed to deliver a continuous stream of dopamine hits by showing content that keeps us scrolling. This can result in users spending hours on social media, often without realizing how much time has passed. Features like infinite scrolling, autoplay videos, and push notifications are specifically designed to keep users hooked. The more time we spend on these platforms, the more data the algorithms can collect, which further refines the personalization of our feeds, making the cycle even more powerful.

AI also influences social interactions by suggesting connections, recommending groups or communities, and predicting what users might want to post about next. While these features can help people find like-minded individuals and foster a sense of community, they can also amplify negative behaviors. For instance, people may feel pressured to present an idealized version of themselves to gain validation through likes and comments, leading to feelings of inadequacy or anxiety. The constant comparison to others' curated lives can impact self-esteem and overall mental well-being.

The Psychological Impact of Algorithmic Feeds

The way algorithms curate and present content on social media has profound psychological effects on users. From the constant pressure to seek validation to the impact of echo chambers on our worldviews, the influence of algorithmic feeds extends into our mental health and behavior.

The Pursuit of Validation and Self-Esteem - One of the most pervasive psychological effects of algorithmic feeds is the impact on self-esteem and the pursuit of validation. Social media platforms are designed to reward content that generates engagement, which often translates to likes, shares, and comments. Users, especially young people, may find themselves constantly seeking approval from their online peers. The number of likes or comments on a post can become a measure of self-worth, leading to anxiety and feelings of inadequacy when a post doesn't perform well. This constant need for validation can affect self-esteem and contribute to a negative self-image.

Additionally, social media often presents a curated and idealized version of reality. People typically share their most exciting experiences, achievements, or happiest moments, creating a distorted view of everyday life. When users compare their own lives to these highlight reels, it can lead to feelings of inadequacy and the false perception that everyone else's life is better or more fulfilling. This phenomenon, known as "social comparison," has been linked to increased rates of anxiety and depression, particularly among teens and young adults.

The Impact of Echo Chambers on Worldviews - Echo chambers created by AI algorithms not only limit exposure to diverse perspectives but also reinforce existing beliefs, making it difficult for users to consider alternative viewpoints. This can have significant consequences for how people perceive the world and engage in social and political discussions. When users are repeatedly exposed to content that aligns with their views, they become more entrenched in their beliefs, and the idea of engaging in open, constructive dialogue with people who hold different opinions becomes less appealing. This polarization can strain relationships and contribute to societal divisions.

Moreover, the psychological effect of echo chambers can extend to how people process information. Repeated exposure to similar content can create a sense of familiarity and acceptance, making it harder to question or critically analyze information. People may become more susceptible to confirmation bias, the tendency to search for, interpret, and remember information in a way that confirms their preexisting beliefs. This can be particularly dangerous when it comes to important topics like politics, health, or social issues, where a lack of diverse perspectives can hinder informed decision-making.

FOMO and the Fear of Missing Out - Algorithmic feeds are also designed to capitalize on the fear of missing out (FOMO). The constant stream of updates, event invitations, and news alerts can make users feel anxious about not being part of something important or exciting. This fear drives people to check their social media accounts repeatedly, further fueling addictive behaviors. FOMO is particularly pronounced on platforms that highlight real-time updates, such as Instagram Stories or Twitter, where content is ephemeral and disappears after a certain period. The pressure to stay constantly connected and engaged can be exhausting and negatively impact overall well-being.

The Spread of Information and Misinformation

One of the most critical issues in the age of algorithm-driven social media is the rapid spread of information—and misinformation. Algorithms are designed to prioritize content that is engaging, but this can lead to the amplification of misleading or false information. The consequences of this are far-reaching, affecting public health, politics, and societal trust.

How Algorithms Amplify Misinformation - Social media algorithms prioritize content that generates high levels of engagement. Unfortunately, false or sensationalized information is often more engaging than factual, nuanced content. Misinformation spreads faster and more widely because it evokes strong emotions, such as fear, anger, or surprise. For example, during a public health crisis, false claims about the safety of vaccines or miracle cures can go viral, leading to real-world consequences. Political misinformation can shape public opinion and even influence elections, undermining the democratic process.

AI algorithms do not have an inherent understanding of truth or accuracy; they are programmed to maximize engagement. This creates a dilemma where content that is misleading but emotionally compelling is given a platform, while accurate but less engaging content may be buried. Fact-checking efforts by social media companies are ongoing, but they often struggle to keep up with the sheer volume of misinformation and the speed at which it spreads.

Echo Chambers and the Reinforcement of False Beliefs - As previously discussed, echo chambers exacerbate the problem of misinformation. When users are repeatedly exposed to content that confirms their beliefs, they become more resistant to correcting misinformation. For example, a person who believes in a conspiracy theory may only see posts that support that theory, making it difficult to accept evidence that contradicts it. This can create a situation where misinformation is not only widespread but also deeply entrenched in certain communities.

Efforts to combat misinformation often face backlash, as attempts to correct false claims can be perceived as censorship or bias. The challenge for social media platforms is to strike a balance between promoting free speech and ensuring that the spread of harmful misinformation is minimized. AI tools are being developed to flag or reduce the visibility of misleading content, but these measures are not foolproof and can sometimes be manipulated or bypassed.

The Role of Users in Mitigating Misinformation

while social media platforms have a responsibility to address the spread of misinformation, users also play a crucial role in mitigating its impact. Critical thinking and media literacy are essential skills in the age of algorithm-driven information. Users need to question the credibility of the content they come across, verify sources, and be aware of the emotional impact that sensational headlines and posts can have. By taking a more skeptical approach to the information they encounter and sharing content responsibly, users can contribute to a more informed and less polarized digital space.

Educational initiatives aimed at teaching people how to recognize misinformation and understand how algorithms influence content consumption are becoming increasingly important. Schools, community organizations, and even social media platforms are beginning to offer resources and workshops focused on media literacy. Understanding how algorithms work can empower users to make more intentional choices about what they engage with and share online.

Collaborative Efforts to Combat Misinformation - Addressing the issue of misinformation requires collaboration between technology companies, governments, researchers, and civil society. Social media platforms have implemented various measures, such as labeling false or misleading content, partnering with fact-checking organizations, and using AI to identify and remove harmful misinformation. However, these efforts are often reactive rather than proactive and can be met with resistance from users who view them as censorship.

Governments and regulatory bodies are also getting involved, exploring legislation to hold platforms accountable for the spread of misinformation. However, such measures must be carefully designed to avoid infringing on free speech rights. Collaboration with independent experts and researchers is crucial to develop balanced approaches that both protect public discourse and prevent the spread of harmful or false information.

The global nature of misinformation adds another layer of complexity. What might be a local issue in one country can quickly become an international concern, as misinformation spreads across borders. This underscores the need for international cooperation and the sharing of best practices to tackle the problem effectively.

Summary of Chapter 9

The age of algorithms has reshaped social interactions, making them more engaging, personalized, and data-driven. AI influences almost every aspect of how we use social media, from the content we see to the ways we seek validation and connect with others. While these technological advancements have made social media a powerful tool for connection and information sharing, they also come with significant drawbacks. The psychological impact of algorithmic feeds, the creation of echo chambers, and the rapid spread of misinformation are challenges that we must address.

Understanding the influence of AI on social media dynamics can empower users to be more intentional and critical in their online behavior. It also highlights the importance of collaborative efforts to create a safer and more informed digital landscape. As we move forward, finding a balance between technological innovation, psychological well-being, and the integrity of information will be essential to shaping the future of social interactions in the age of algorithms.

Chapter 10. Emotional Intelligence and AI Companions

As artificial intelligence (AI) technology continues to evolve, its ability to engage with humans on an emotional level is becoming increasingly sophisticated. AI companions, designed to simulate human-like interactions and provide emotional support, are being integrated into various aspects of our lives. From virtual friends and mental health chatbots to emotionally intelligent assistants, these AI systems aim to meet our emotional and social needs in a world that is more connected yet often more isolated. However, these advancements raise important questions about the ethics of emotional AI and the potential consequences for human connection and well-being. This chapter provides an in-depth look at virtual companions, the role of AI in emotional support, and the ethical challenges surrounding AI-emotional interfaces.

Virtual Companions and Human Connection

Virtual companions, powered by AI, are designed to simulate real human conversations and interactions, offering companionship and emotional engagement to users. These AI companions are used in various contexts, from providing company to elderly individuals and helping children develop social skills to offering conversational practice for language learners or just being a digital confidant for people of all ages. The goal is to create an experience that feels authentic and emotionally engaging.

The Technology Behind Virtual Companions - Virtual companions use a combination of natural language processing (NLP), machine learning, and emotional recognition technologies to understand and respond to users in a meaningful way. These AI systems can process and interpret language, analyze sentiment, and recognize cues such as voice tone, facial expressions, or text patterns to determine how the user is feeling. For instance, if a user's voice sounds strained or their text contains words that indicate sadness, the AI companion may respond with comforting or empathetic words. Advanced AI companions can adapt to the user's communication style over time, making conversations feel more personal and relevant.

A key feature of AI companions is their ability to provide a sense of companionship and combat loneliness. For example, an elderly person living alone may benefit from having an AI companion that checks in on them, engages in light conversation, and even helps with reminders about taking medication or staying active. For younger users, AI companions can serve as friendly, nonjudgmental entities that provide a safe space for expressing feelings or practicing social skills. These companions are especially useful for individuals who struggle with social anxiety or have difficulty forming connections in the real world.

However, while AI companions can offer a sense of connection, they cannot fully replicate the depth and complexity of human relationships. Critics argue that relying too much on virtual companions may exacerbate feelings of isolation rather than alleviate them, as users may become more accustomed to interacting with AI than with real people. The impact of virtual companions on social well-being and human connection is a subject of ongoing research, and it raises questions about how these technologies should be integrated into society.

The Role of AI in Emotional Support

AI has emerged as a tool for providing emotional support, offering a new way to assist people in managing stress, anxiety, and other emotional challenges. These AI-driven systems range from simple chatbots that help with daily stressors to advanced platforms that use therapeutic techniques to offer more structured emotional support. AI in this context aims to be accessible, nonjudgmental, and always available, providing users with immediate assistance when needed.

AI-Powered Mental Health and Wellness Apps - One of the most impactful applications of AI in emotional support is in mental health and wellness apps. These apps use AI to engage in text-based or voice-based conversations, checking in on how the user is feeling and offering guidance, coping strategies, or mindfulness exercises. For example, apps like Woebot and Wysa use cognitive-behavioral therapy (CBT) principles to help users reframe negative thoughts and practice healthier ways of thinking. These AI companions can provide emotional validation and suggest activities to improve well-being, such as breathing exercises or guided meditation.

AI-powered mental health platforms are also used in more structured therapeutic contexts. Virtual reality (VR) therapy is being developed to help people overcome phobias, manage PTSD, or practice social skills. In these scenarios, AI-driven systems create a personalized and adaptive experience. For example, a person with a fear of heights can be guided through a VR experience that gradually exposes them to higher elevations while an AI algorithm monitors their physiological responses and adjusts the difficulty level accordingly.

AI emotional support systems are especially beneficial for people who may not have access to traditional therapy, whether due to cost, location, or stigma. They can provide a form of care that is immediate and accessible 24/7. However, these systems also come with limitations. AI, no matter how advanced, lacks the genuine empathy, intuition, and nuanced understanding of a human therapist. For individuals dealing with severe mental health issues, relying solely on AI support can be insufficient or even dangerous. Human therapists provide a level of care and understanding that AI cannot replicate, and they are trained to handle complex situations that may arise during therapy.

The Balance between AI and Human Support - The most effective use of AI in emotional support may be as a supplement to human care rather than a replacement. For example, AI can help monitor a patient's progress between therapy sessions or provide daily emotional check-ins, while a human therapist handles more complex issues and provides personalized care. The combination of AI and human support can create a comprehensive mental health care model that is both effective and accessible.

Ethical Challenges in AI-Emotional Interfaces

The use of AI in emotionally sensitive contexts brings up a range of ethical challenges that must be carefully considered. As AI systems become better at understanding and responding to human emotions, the line between genuine and artificial empathy becomes increasingly blurred. Additionally, concerns about privacy, dependency, and the potential for emotional manipulation are important issues that must be addressed to ensure the responsible use of AI-emotional interfaces.

Privacy and Security of Emotional Data - AI systems that provide emotional support often collect and analyze deeply personal and sensitive data. This data can include a user's mental health history, emotional patterns, and even physiological responses. The collection of such data raises serious concerns about privacy and security. A data breach could have devastating consequences, as it would expose information that is not only private but also highly sensitive. Users must be able to trust that their data is being handled securely and ethically, with clear policies about how their information is stored, used, and shared.

Developers of AI-emotional interfaces need to implement robust security measures, such as end-to-end encryption and secure data storage, to protect user privacy. Transparency is also crucial. Users should be fully informed about what data is being collected, how it will be used, and who has access to it. Regulations and guidelines, similar to those used for medical data, may be necessary to ensure that emotional AI systems adhere to high ethical standards.

Authenticity and the Illusion of Empathy - One of the most significant ethical concerns with AI-emotional interfaces is the authenticity of the emotional responses generated by these systems. While AI can simulate empathy by using algorithms to recognize and respond to emotions, it does not genuinely feel or understand those emotions. This raises questions about the ethical implications of creating machines that mimic human feelings. If users become emotionally attached to AI companions, believing them to be genuinely caring, it could lead to emotional confusion and an unhealthy reliance on artificial relationships.

The illusion of empathy can also be problematic if it is used for manipulative purposes. For instance, emotionally aware AI systems could be designed to influence users' behavior or make them more susceptible to marketing tactics. An AI system that detects when a user is feeling vulnerable could be programmed to push products or services that promise comfort or relief. This type of emotional manipulation is a serious ethical issue that requires strict regulation and oversight to prevent abuse.

Dependency and the Impact on Real-World Relationships - Another ethical challenge is the risk of dependency on AI companions for emotional support. If people start to rely heavily on AI for emotional connection, it could weaken their real-world relationships and social skills. This is particularly concerning for young people, who are still developing their social and emotional intelligence. The more time individuals spend interacting with AI, the less time they may invest in building meaningful human connections. While AI companions can be valuable tools for certain situations, they should not replace genuine human interaction.

Designers of AI-emotional interfaces must consider the long-term impact of these technologies on social behavior and human well-being. Encouraging a healthy balance between digital and real-world interactions is crucial. Additionally, there should be measures in place to ensure that AI systems are used to complement, not replace, human support networks.

Regulation and Ethical Oversight - To address these ethical concerns, there is a need for regulation and ethical oversight.

Governments, tech companies, and ethical boards must work together to create guidelines that ensure AI-emotional interfaces are used responsibly. This includes setting standards for data privacy, preventing emotional manipulation, and ensuring that AI systems are designed with the well-being of users in mind. Involving psychologists, ethicists, and community representatives in the design and implementation of AI-emotional interfaces is essential to address these concerns from multiple perspectives. For example, ethical boards could review AI systems to ensure they meet stringent guidelines before they are released to the public. Collaboration between industry leaders and regulatory bodies can also establish frameworks that prioritize user safety and emotional well-being.

Another aspect of ethical oversight involves transparency and accountability. Developers should be clear about the capabilities and limitations of AI-emotional interfaces, making sure that users understand that these systems, while helpful, do not replace professional human support. Additionally, AI systems should have built-in mechanisms for users to provide feedback or report issues, and companies should be held accountable for the impact of their technology on users' mental and emotional health.

Overall, the future of AI-emotional interfaces holds great promise, but it also demands a careful balance between technological advancement and the ethical considerations that come with interacting with human emotions. As AI continues to evolve, ongoing dialogue and research will be crucial to understanding the full impact of these systems and ensuring they are used in ways that genuinely benefit society.

Summary of Chapter 10

The integration of emotional intelligence into AI systems is opening up new possibilities for companionship, emotional support, and mental health assistance. Virtual companions can provide comfort and engagement for those who are isolated, and AI-powered mental health apps are making emotional support more accessible. However, the use of AI in such deeply personal and emotional contexts comes with significant ethical challenges. Concerns about data privacy, the authenticity of AI-generated empathy, and the risk of social dependency must be carefully managed.

As AI becomes more emotionally aware, it is crucial to establish clear ethical guidelines and regulatory frameworks that protect users and promote responsible use. Balancing technological innovation with human values such as trust, privacy, and genuine connection will be essential to ensure that AI-emotional interfaces are a force for good in society. By fostering collaboration between developers, psychologists, ethicists, and policymakers, we can harness the potential of AI to improve emotional well-being while safeguarding against its possible pitfalls.

Chapter 11. Bias and Fairness in AI Systems

Artificial intelligence (AI) systems are increasingly being used to make important decisions in various sectors, such as healthcare, hiring, criminal justice, education, and lending. While AI has the potential to improve efficiency and decision-making, it also comes with the risk of bias, which can lead to unfair and discriminatory outcomes. Understanding the causes of bias in algorithms, exploring strategies to mitigate it, and examining the social impact of AI-driven decisions are crucial steps toward creating fairer AI systems. This chapter provides an in-depth exploration of bias and fairness in AI, highlighting the complexities and the critical need for equitable practices.

Understanding Bias in Algorithms

Bias in AI algorithms occurs when these systems produce results that are systematically prejudiced due to flaws in the data, the design of the algorithm, or the way the AI system interacts with users. Bias in AI is not merely a technical issue; it often reflects broader societal inequalities. Understanding the different types of bias and how they arise is essential for addressing the problem.

Types of Bias in AI Systems

1. **Data Bias**: Data bias is one of the most common sources of bias in AI. It occurs when the data used to train the algorithm is not representative of the population it is meant to serve. For instance, if a facial recognition system is trained predominantly on images of lighter-skinned individuals, it may perform poorly when recognizing faces with darker skin tones. Similarly, if an AI system designed to predict job performance is trained on historical hiring data that favors men, it may discriminate against female candidates. Data bias can result from historical inequalities, sampling errors, or a lack of diversity in the data.

2. **Algorithmic Bias**: Algorithmic bias occurs when the design or structure of the algorithm introduces unfairness. This can happen even if the data itself is relatively unbiased. For example, an algorithm that prioritizes certain features over others may inadvertently favor specific groups. If an AI system used for lending decisions gives more weight to credit history and income without considering contextual factors, it could disadvantage individuals from lower-income backgrounds, perpetuating existing disparities. Algorithmic bias can also arise from optimization goals that prioritize accuracy or efficiency over fairness.

3. **Interaction Bias**: Interaction bias occurs when an AI system learns from user behavior in ways that reinforce existing biases. For instance, social media algorithms prioritize content that generates high engagement, which can lead to the amplification of sensational or biased content. Over time, these algorithms may create echo chambers, where users are exposed only to information that aligns with their beliefs, further entrenching biases. Similarly, AI-powered recommendation systems can reinforce stereotypes by suggesting content based on biased user interactions.

Real-World Examples of AI Bias - AI bias has been observed in various real-world applications, often with significant consequences. For example:

- **Hiring Algorithms**: Several companies have used AI to streamline the hiring process, but these systems have been found to favor male candidates if they were trained on biased data that reflected historical gender disparities in hiring practices. In some cases, AI systems penalized resumes that contained indicators of female identity, such as mentions of women's organizations.
- **Criminal Justice Systems**: AI algorithms used in criminal justice, such as risk assessment tools for predicting recidivism, have been criticized for being biased against minority groups. These tools often rely on data from past arrests and convictions, which may reflect biased policing practices, leading to unfair outcomes and perpetuating systemic inequalities.
- **Healthcare Algorithms**: AI systems used in healthcare have shown biases in predicting which patients should receive more intensive care. For example, an algorithm designed to allocate

healthcare resources was found to be biased against Black patients because it used healthcare costs as a proxy for medical need. Since Black patients historically receive less healthcare, the algorithm underestimated their level of risk.

Understanding these examples helps to illustrate the real-world implications of AI bias and the importance of developing more equitable systems.

Strategies to Mitigate AI Bias

Mitigating bias in AI systems is a complex challenge that requires a holistic approach. Addressing bias involves improving data practices, designing fairness-aware algorithms, and implementing ongoing monitoring and evaluation. These strategies are essential to create AI systems that make fair and unbiased decisions.

Data Preprocessing and Diversity - One of the first steps in reducing AI bias is to improve the quality and diversity of the data used to train algorithms. Data preprocessing involves cleaning and balancing datasets to ensure they are representative of the population the AI system is intended to serve. Techniques like oversampling underrepresented groups or using synthetic data to fill gaps can help mitigate data bias. For example, if an AI system is being developed for facial recognition, it should be trained on a diverse set of images that includes people of different races, ages, and genders to reduce performance disparities.

However, it's important to note that data preprocessing must be done carefully to avoid introducing new biases. Additionally, simply removing sensitive attributes like race or gender from the data is not always sufficient, as other correlated features (e.g., ZIP codes or names) may still act as proxies for those attributes. Developers need to be aware of these potential pitfalls and use techniques like reweighting or stratified sampling to achieve a more balanced dataset.

Fairness-Aware Algorithm Design - Another crucial strategy for mitigating bias is to design algorithms with fairness in mind. Fairness-aware machine learning techniques can help ensure that algorithms make equitable decisions. One approach is to modify the objective function of the algorithm to include fairness constraints. For example, an algorithm used to determine loan eligibility could be designed to minimize disparate impact, ensuring that approval rates are more equitable across different demographic groups.

Fairness metrics, such as demographic parity, equalized odds, and disparate impact ratio, can be used to evaluate the performance of the algorithm and ensure it meets fairness criteria. Demographic parity requires that outcomes be equally distributed across groups, while equalized odds ensure that the algorithm has equal true positive and false positive rates for all groups. Developers can use these metrics to identify and correct biases, balancing fairness with other performance goals.

Ongoing Auditing and Ethical Oversight - AI systems are not static; they evolve and adapt over time, which means that bias can develop or change as the system learns from new data. Regular auditing and continuous monitoring are essential to ensure that AI systems remain fair and unbiased. This can involve periodic reviews of the algorithm's performance, independent audits by third-party organizations, and the use of bias-detection tools. Transparency and accountability are also key components of ethical oversight. AI systems should come with clear documentation about how they work, what data they use, and what measures have been taken to mitigate bias.

Involving diverse teams in the development and auditing process is another effective way to identify and address bias. A diverse group of developers, ethicists, and social scientists can bring different perspectives and insights, making it more likely that potential biases will be detected and mitigated. Collaboration with affected communities and stakeholders can also help ensure that the AI system is aligned with the needs and values of those it impacts.

The Social Impact of Algorithmic Decisions

The decisions made by AI systems can have profound social consequences, affecting people's lives in ways that are both visible and invisible. When AI algorithms are used to make high-stakes decisions—such as who gets a job, who qualifies for a loan, or who is considered a risk in the criminal justice system—these decisions can reinforce or exacerbate existing social inequalities. Understanding the social impact of algorithmic decisions is crucial for creating AI systems that are fair and just.

Impact on Marginalized Communities - AI bias often disproportionately affects marginalized communities, exacerbating existing disparities in areas like employment, healthcare, and law enforcement. For example, an AI system used to screen job applicants may inadvertently disadvantage candidates from certain racial or gender groups if it is trained on biased historical data. This can make it even harder for underrepresented groups to access employment opportunities, perpetuating cycles of inequality.

In healthcare, biased algorithms can lead to disparities in the quality of care received by different groups. If an AI system is less accurate in diagnosing certain conditions in women or minority patients, it can contribute to unequal health outcomes. Similarly, in the criminal justice system, biased risk assessment tools can lead to harsher sentencing for minority defendants, perpetuating systemic racism and eroding trust in the justice system.

Economic and Societal Implications - The use of biased AI systems can also have broader economic and societal implications. For instance, if AI systems systematically discriminate against certain groups in lending or hiring, it can contribute to wealth inequality and limit economic mobility. Biased algorithms can also undermine public trust in technology, leading to skepticism and resistance to AI adoption. When people feel that AI systems are unfair or biased, it can deepen societal divisions and create backlash against technological advancements.

The Role of Accountability and Governance

addressing the social impact of algorithmic decisions requires strong governance and accountability mechanisms. Policymakers, technology companies, and civil society organizations must work together to establish regulations that promote fairness and transparency in AI systems. These regulations should ensure that AI is used in ways that benefit society and do not reinforce existing inequalities. For example, laws could mandate that companies conduct regular bias audits of their AI systems and disclose the results publicly. Government agencies could also set standards for algorithmic accountability, requiring organizations to explain how their AI systems make decisions, particularly in high-stakes scenarios like hiring or criminal justice.

Another important aspect of governance is the establishment of ethical guidelines for AI development and deployment. These guidelines can help ensure that AI systems are designed and used responsibly, with a focus on minimizing harm and promoting equitable outcomes. Engaging diverse stakeholders in the creation and oversight of these guidelines, including those who are most affected by AI decisions, is essential for creating systems that reflect the values and needs of society as a whole.

Public Awareness and Education - Increasing public awareness about how AI systems work and the potential biases they can introduce is also crucial. Educating people about the risks and benefits of AI empowers them to advocate for more ethical and fair AI practices. Public education campaigns and community workshops can help demystify AI and make the technology more understandable and accessible. People should be informed about how algorithmic decisions can impact their lives and what rights they have when it comes to AI-based decisions.

Moreover, encouraging open dialogue between technologists, policymakers, and the public can foster a more inclusive approach to AI development. People from all backgrounds should have the opportunity to voice their concerns and contribute to the conversation about how AI should be used. This collaborative approach can lead to more robust and equitable AI systems that serve the common good.

Summary of Chapter 11

Bias and fairness in AI systems are critical issues that have far-reaching implications for individuals and society. Bias in algorithms can arise from data that reflects historical inequalities, flawed design choices, or user interactions that reinforce stereotypes. Understanding these sources of bias is essential for creating more equitable AI systems. Strategies to mitigate bias include improving data diversity, designing fairness-aware algorithms, and implementing continuous monitoring and ethical oversight.

The social impact of algorithmic decisions is significant, especially for marginalized communities, who are often disproportionately affected by biased AI systems. Addressing these challenges requires collaboration between policymakers, technologists, and civil society to establish regulations and ethical guidelines that promote fairness and transparency. Public awareness and education are also crucial for empowering people to understand and engage with AI technology.

As AI continues to shape our world, ensuring that it is used in a fair and just manner will be essential. By taking a proactive approach to address bias and promote fairness, we can harness the power of AI to create positive social change and improve the lives of people across all demographics.

Chapter 12. AI and Ethical Decision-Making

The rise of artificial intelligence (AI) has brought about significant advancements across various fields, from healthcare and transportation to education and finance. However, with this tremendous potential comes the responsibility to address the ethical dilemmas that arise from AI's use and implementation. Ethical decision-making in AI is about ensuring that AI technologies are designed, deployed, and used in ways that uphold moral values, minimize harm, and promote fairness and human well-being. This chapter provides a comprehensive exploration of what ethics means in the context of AI, examines case studies that highlight ethical challenges, and discusses how to develop frameworks that ensure ethical AI practices.

Defining Ethics in Artificial Intelligence

Understanding ethics in the context of artificial intelligence requires a clear definition of what constitutes ethical behavior for machines. AI ethics revolves around ensuring that AI systems adhere to moral principles that align with human values. These principles guide how AI systems are built and used, focusing on protecting human rights, promoting fairness, and preventing harm.

Core Ethical Principles in AI

1. **Transparency**: Transparency in AI means making the decision-making processes of AI systems understandable and clear to all stakeholders. When AI makes decisions that impact people's lives—such as approving a loan, diagnosing a medical condition, or suggesting legal actions—those affected should have access to an explanation of how and why the AI made its decision. Transparency also involves documenting the sources of data, the algorithms used, and the measures taken to prevent bias. It ensures that AI systems are not "black boxes" but rather accountable and open to scrutiny.

2. **Fairness**: Fairness is a crucial aspect of ethical AI. An AI system must treat all individuals and groups equitably, without discrimination based on race, gender, age, socioeconomic status, or other attributes. However, achieving fairness is complex, as AI systems often learn from historical data that may reflect existing social biases. Developers must actively work to identify and mitigate these biases to ensure that AI systems do not reinforce or amplify inequality. Fairness also involves creating algorithms that consider diverse populations and ensure that AI technologies benefit everyone, not just a privileged few.

3. **Accountability**: Accountability means that there must be

mechanisms in place to hold people or organizations responsible for the actions of AI systems. When an AI system makes a mistake or causes harm, it should be clear who is accountable—whether it is the developers, the company deploying the system, or the policymakers who regulate it. Establishing accountability is essential for building trust in AI and ensuring that there are consequences for unethical behavior or negligence.

4. **Privacy**: Privacy is another fundamental ethical principle in AI. AI systems often rely on large amounts of personal data to function effectively, raising concerns about how this data is collected, stored, and used. Ethical AI practices must ensure that user data is protected and that individuals have control over their personal information. This includes obtaining informed consent, anonymizing data when possible, and implementing robust security measures to prevent data breaches.

5. **Beneficence and Non-Maleficence**: These principles come from bioethics and emphasize doing well (beneficence) and avoiding harm (non-maleficence). AI systems should be designed to improve human well-being and avoid causing physical, psychological, or social harm. For example, in healthcare, AI should enhance patient outcomes without putting patients at unnecessary risk. In social contexts, AI should not promote harmful behaviors or spread misinformation.

By adhering to these principles, AI developers and policymakers can ensure that AI systems contribute positively to society while minimizing the risks and negative impacts associated with their use.

Case Studies of Ethical AI Challenges

Examining real-world case studies of ethical challenges in AI can provide valuable insights into the complexities and consequences of ethical decision-making. These examples highlight situations where AI systems failed to meet ethical standards, causing harm or sparking controversy. Understanding these cases can help developers and policymakers learn from past mistakes and work toward more ethical AI practices.

Case Study 1: Biased Hiring Algorithms

A major tech company developed an AI system to help streamline the hiring process by screening resumes and ranking candidates. However, the algorithm was later found to be biased against women. This happened because the training data consisted primarily of resumes from male candidates, reflecting the company's historical hiring practices. As a result, the AI system penalized resumes that contained terms associated with women, such as mentions of women's sports teams or all-female colleges. The algorithm reinforced gender inequality rather than promoting a fair hiring process.

Ethical Implications: This case highlights the importance of fairness and the need to eliminate bias in AI systems. It also underscores the ethical responsibility of companies to audit and test their AI systems for potential biases before deployment. The lack of diverse and representative training data led to unfair outcomes, which could have been mitigated with better data practices and fairness-aware algorithm design.

Case Study 2: Predictive Policing and Racial Bias

In several cities, police departments have used predictive policing algorithms to forecast crime hotspots and allocate law enforcement resources. However, investigations revealed that these algorithms disproportionately targeted minority neighborhoods. The algorithms were trained on historical crime data, which reflected years of biased policing practices. As a result, predictive policing systems perpetuated racial bias, leading to over-policing in communities of color and exacerbating tensions between law enforcement and residents.

Ethical Implications: This case illustrates the importance of accountability and the social impact of AI decisions. The use of biased data led to discriminatory practices, raising questions about whether such systems should be used at all. It also demonstrates the need for community involvement and transparency when deploying AI in public safety settings. Ethical guidelines and oversight are crucial to prevent AI from perpetuating systemic injustices.

Case Study 3: Facial Recognition and Privacy Concerns

Several governments and companies have deployed facial recognition technology in public spaces, raising significant privacy concerns. In some instances, facial recognition systems have been used without the knowledge or consent of the people being monitored. Additionally, research has shown that these systems often perform poorly on people with darker skin tones, leading to higher rates of misidentification and wrongful accusations. The use of facial recognition in law enforcement has sparked widespread debate about the balance between security and civil liberties.

Ethical Implications: This case highlights the ethical principles of privacy, transparency, and non-maleficence. The use of facial recognition technology without informed consent violates individuals' privacy rights. The inaccuracies in the technology also pose a risk of harm, especially to marginalized communities. Policymakers must weigh the benefits of facial recognition against the potential for abuse and ensure that robust regulations are in place to protect citizens.

Developing Frameworks for Ethical AI

Creating ethical AI frameworks involves establishing guidelines and standards that ensure AI systems align with human values and do not cause harm. These frameworks are essential for developers, companies, and policymakers to navigate the ethical complexities of AI and make informed decisions. Developing robust ethical AI frameworks requires collaboration, accountability, and a commitment to ongoing evaluation.

Components of an Ethical AI Framework

1. **Ethical Guidelines**: Ethical guidelines provide a set of principles that AI developers and organizations must follow. These guidelines can be created by governments, professional organizations, or companies themselves. They outline what is considered acceptable and unacceptable behavior for AI systems. For example, an ethical AI framework might include rules about not using AI for surveillance without informed consent, or ensuring that AI systems are designed to avoid discrimination.

2. **Impact Assessments**: Before deploying an AI system, organizations should conduct ethical impact assessments to evaluate the potential risks and benefits. This assessment should consider the social, economic, and psychological impacts of the AI system, especially on vulnerable populations. By identifying potential harms early, developers can take steps to mitigate them. For example, an AI system used in healthcare should be assessed for whether it provides equitable treatment to all patient groups, including those who have historically been underserved.

3. **Transparency and Explainability**: An ethical AI framework must emphasize the importance of transparency and

explainability. This means providing clear documentation about how the AI system works, what data it uses, and how decisions are made. Explainability is especially important in high-stakes situations, such as criminal justice or healthcare, where people need to understand and trust AI decisions. If an AI system denies someone a loan or recommends a medical treatment, the affected individuals should be able to get an explanation of the decision-making process.

4. **Accountability Mechanisms**: Establishing accountability mechanisms ensures that there are consequences when AI systems cause harm or violate ethical guidelines. This includes creating oversight bodies that can investigate complaints, enforce regulations, and hold organizations responsible. Accountability also involves having clear lines of responsibility within organizations, so it is known who is in charge of monitoring and maintaining the ethical use of AI.

Collaboration and Inclusive Decision-Making - Developing ethical AI frameworks requires collaboration among diverse stakeholders, including technologists, ethicists, policymakers, and representatives from affected communities. An inclusive approach ensures that multiple perspectives are considered, leading to more robust and comprehensive frameworks. For instance, involving community representatives and advocacy groups in the design and implementation of AI systems can help identify potential ethical concerns that developers might overlook. By including a range of voices, organizations can create AI systems that are more equitable and better aligned with societal values.

Collaboration also extends to cross-industry and international cooperation. AI is a global technology, and its impact transcends national borders. As such, developing standardized ethical guidelines that apply across different countries and sectors can help establish a consistent approach to ethical AI. Initiatives like international AI ethics councils and conferences can facilitate the sharing of best practices and the development of universal ethical principles.

Continuous Monitoring and Adaptation - Ethical AI frameworks must be adaptable and subject to continuous monitoring. As AI technologies evolve and new ethical challenges emerge, frameworks need to be updated to remain relevant. Continuous monitoring involves regularly assessing the performance and impact of AI systems, collecting feedback from users and affected communities, and making necessary adjustments. This process helps ensure that AI systems remain fair, transparent, and accountable over time.

Organizations should also be prepared to learn from mistakes and improve their practices. When ethical issues arise, it is essential to conduct thorough investigations, share findings transparently, and implement corrective actions. A culture of learning and accountability can help prevent future ethical failures and build public trust in AI technologies.

Summary of Chapter 12

Ethical decision-making in AI is a critical area that addresses the complex moral dilemmas posed by the widespread use of AI technologies. Defining ethics in AI involves understanding core principles such as transparency, fairness, accountability, privacy, and the commitment to do well while avoiding harm. Case studies of ethical AI challenges, such as biased hiring algorithms, predictive policing, and facial recognition technology, provide valuable lessons about the consequences of ethical failures and the importance of proactive measures.

Developing frameworks for ethical AI requires a comprehensive approach that includes ethical guidelines, impact assessments, transparency, and accountability mechanisms. Collaboration among diverse stakeholders and continuous monitoring are essential for adapting to new ethical challenges and ensuring that AI systems remain aligned with societal values. By fostering a culture of ethical responsibility, we can harness the power of AI to improve lives while upholding human rights and promoting social good.

Chapter 13. Data Security in an Algorithmic World

As artificial intelligence (AI) continues to shape industries and influence various aspects of our daily lives, the security and protection of data have become increasingly important. AI systems are only as effective as the data they rely on, which means vast amounts of personal, financial, and proprietary information are collected and processed. However, this heavy reliance on data also introduces significant security risks. In this chapter, we explore the vulnerabilities that AI systems face, the critical role of encryption in protecting data, and the global policies that govern data security in our interconnected world.

Data Protection and AI Vulnerabilities

AI systems rely on massive datasets to perform tasks ranging from image recognition and natural language processing to predictive analytics. However, the use of large volumes of data makes AI systems susceptible to various security threats. Understanding these vulnerabilities is essential for developing effective data protection strategies and ensuring that sensitive information remains secure.

AI Data Vulnerabilities

1. **Data Breaches**: One of the most pressing concerns in an AI-driven world is the risk of data breaches. AI systems often store and process sensitive personal information, such as social security numbers, medical records, financial data, and biometric details. Hackers and cybercriminals target these systems because a single breach can expose the data of millions of users. Data breaches can lead to identity theft, financial losses, reputational damage, and even physical harm in cases where health or safety information is compromised. As AI systems become more sophisticated and interconnected, the potential impact of data breaches grows, making robust data protection measures a top priority.

Example: In healthcare, AI systems analyze patient data to improve diagnoses and treatment plans. If a hacker were to access and leak this data, it could have devastating consequences for patients, including the unauthorized disclosure of medical conditions and personal details. Organizations must implement stringent cybersecurity measures to safeguard sensitive data and protect patient privacy.

1. **Data Poisoning**: Data poisoning attacks are a unique and concerning vulnerability in AI systems. These attacks occur when malicious actors intentionally tamper with the training data used to teach AI models. By inserting false, misleading, or corrupted information into the dataset, attackers can manipulate the behavior of the AI system. For example, if a facial recognition AI is trained on a poisoned dataset that contains altered images, it may misidentify people or make biased decisions. Data poisoning can have serious consequences, particularly in high-stakes applications like autonomous vehicles, financial trading, or national security.

Example: Consider a self-driving car that relies on an AI system trained to recognize road signs. If attackers poison the training data by altering images of stop signs to resemble speed limit signs, the car could fail to stop at intersections, putting passengers and pedestrians at risk. Ensuring the integrity and quality of training data is crucial to prevent such attacks and maintain the safety and reliability of AI systems.

1. **Model Inversion Attacks**: Model inversion is a sophisticated attack in which adversaries attempt to reverse-engineer an AI model to extract sensitive information about the data it was trained on. Even if the original data is not explicitly stored, attackers can use model inversion techniques to reconstruct aspects of the training data. For instance, if an AI system is trained on a dataset of facial images, attackers could use the model's outputs to infer or recreate images of individuals' faces. This poses significant privacy risks, as it means that private or personal data could be compromised even when proper data anonymization techniques are in place.

Example: In a financial AI system that predicts credit scores, attackers could perform a model inversion attack to extract information about individuals' financial habits, such as their income levels, spending patterns, or outstanding debts. This type of attack underscores the need for privacy-preserving techniques in AI model design to prevent unauthorized access to sensitive information.

Understanding these vulnerabilities highlights the importance of developing robust data protection measures. AI developers and organizations must prioritize data security at every stage of the AI lifecycle, from data collection and storage to model training and deployment.

The Role of Encryption in AI Systems

Encryption is a fundamental component of data security, playing a crucial role in protecting information from unauthorized access. As AI systems handle increasingly sensitive and valuable data, encryption techniques are essential for ensuring that this data remains secure, both at rest and in transit. Encryption transforms data into a format that can only be read or processed by someone with the appropriate decryption key, making it more difficult for attackers to access or exploit the data.

Types of Encryption Used in AI Systems

1. **Data Encryption at Rest**: Data encryption at rest refers to protecting data that is stored on devices or servers. This type of encryption ensures that even if a hacker gains access to the storage system, they cannot read the data without the decryption key. AI systems often store large volumes of data, such as user profiles, transaction histories, or medical records, making encryption at rest a critical security measure. Techniques like Advanced Encryption Standard (AES) are commonly used to encrypt data stored in databases, data warehouses, and cloud storage.

   Example: In a banking AI system that analyzes customer transactions to detect fraud, all transaction data stored in the database should be encrypted. If a cybercriminal were to breach the bank's servers, they would only encounter encrypted information, which would be unreadable without the proper keys. This adds an additional layer of protection and helps safeguard sensitive financial data.

1. **Data Encryption in Transit**: Data encryption in transit refers to securing data as it moves between different systems or

networks. Since AI systems often communicate with other devices, such as sending data between a server and a mobile app, encryption in transit is vital to prevent interception by malicious actors. Secure communication protocols, such as Transport Layer Security (TLS), are used to encrypt data during transmission, ensuring that sensitive information remains confidential.

Example: When a user interacts with an AI-powered healthcare chatbot and shares medical symptoms, the data transmitted between the user's device and the server must be encrypted. Encryption in transit ensures that no one can intercept or eavesdrop on this communication, protecting the user's privacy and preventing data theft.

1. **Homomorphic Encryption**: Homomorphic encryption is an advanced technique that allows AI systems to perform computations on encrypted data without needing to decrypt it. This is particularly useful for privacy-preserving AI applications, such as analyzing medical data or performing financial calculations. With homomorphic encryption, sensitive data can be processed securely, ensuring that privacy is maintained even during data analysis.

Example: In a collaborative healthcare research project, multiple hospitals may want to share patient data to train an AI model while keeping the data private. Homomorphic encryption enables the AI system to analyze the encrypted data without exposing the underlying patient information. This allows researchers to benefit from shared insights while protecting patient confidentiality.

Encryption is a powerful tool for securing data in AI systems, but it must be implemented correctly and combined with other security measures to provide comprehensive protection. As AI continues to evolve, new encryption methods and privacy-enhancing technologies will be needed to keep pace with emerging threats.

Global Policies for Data Security

As data security becomes a global concern, governments and international organizations have implemented policies and regulations to protect personal and sensitive information. These policies aim to set standards for data protection, promote transparency, and ensure that organizations handling data are held accountable for security breaches. Understanding these global policies is crucial for organizations that operate internationally and use AI to process data from various jurisdictions.

Key Data Security Regulations

1. **General Data Protection Regulation (GDPR):** The GDPR is one of the most comprehensive data protection laws in the world, enacted by the European Union (EU) in 2018. It sets strict guidelines for how organizations collect, store, and process personal data. The GDPR requires organizations to obtain explicit consent from individuals before collecting their data, provide transparency about how data is used, and implement robust security measures to protect data. Non-compliance can result in hefty fines, making GDPR compliance a top priority for companies operating in the EU.

Example: An AI company that offers a personalized fitness app to users in Europe must comply with GDPR regulations. This means informing users about how their fitness data will be used, ensuring data encryption, and allowing users to delete their data if they choose. The company must also be prepared to report any data breaches to the relevant authorities within 72 hours.

1. **California Consumer Privacy Act (CCPA):** The CCPA,

enacted in 2020, is a state-level data privacy law in the United States that grants California residents more control over their personal data. It gives consumers the right to know what data is being collected about them, request the deletion of their data, and opt out of the sale of their data. The CCPA also requires businesses to implement reasonable security measures to protect data from breaches.

Example: A social media company using AI to analyze user behavior for targeted advertising must comply with the CCPA if it operates in California. This includes allowing users to opt out of having their data sold and providing clear disclosures about data collection practices. If the company experiences a data breach, it must notify affected users and take steps to mitigate the impact. Failure to comply with CCPA requirements can result in significant fines and legal consequences.

1. **Health Insurance Portability and Accountability Act (HIPAA)**: HIPAA is a U.S. regulation that sets standards for the protection of sensitive patient health information. Healthcare organizations that use AI for tasks such as diagnosing illnesses or managing patient records must ensure that all data is securely handled in accordance with HIPAA guidelines. This includes encrypting health information, limiting access to authorized personnel, and regularly auditing data security practices.

   Example: A hospital that uses an AI system to predict patient outcomes must implement stringent security measures to protect patient data. The AI system should encrypt medical records and follow protocols for data access and handling. If a breach occurs, the hospital must report it to affected individuals and federal authorities.

The Need for International Collaboration

Data security is a global issue, and international collaboration is essential for creating consistent standards and addressing cross-border data flows. Organizations that operate internationally often face challenges in navigating different data protection laws and ensuring compliance in multiple jurisdictions. Efforts such as the development of international data protection frameworks, like the OECD Guidelines on the Protection of Privacy, aim to harmonize regulations and facilitate the safe transfer of data between countries.

Emerging Trends in Global Data Security Policies

As technology evolves, so do data security threats. Governments and organizations are increasingly focusing on emerging trends such as:

- **AI-Specific Regulations**: Some countries are exploring regulations specifically aimed at the ethical and secure use of AI, including guidelines for data security in AI applications. These regulations may address issues like data anonymization, secure AI model sharing, and accountability for AI-driven data breaches.

- **Cross-Border Data Agreements**: International agreements, such as the EU-U.S. Privacy Shield (which has since been invalidated but paved the way for new data transfer frameworks), play a crucial role in governing the flow of data across borders. These agreements set standards for how data is protected when transferred internationally.

Summary of Chapter 13

Data security is a critical issue in an algorithmic world, where AI systems rely on vast amounts of data to operate effectively. Understanding the vulnerabilities associated with AI, such as data breaches, data poisoning, and model inversion attacks, is essential for developing robust protection strategies. Encryption plays a vital role in securing data, both at rest and in transit, and advanced techniques like homomorphic encryption are paving the way for more secure AI applications.

Global data security policies, such as GDPR, CCPA, and HIPAA, set standards for data protection and ensure accountability for organizations that handle sensitive information. As AI continues to evolve, international collaboration and the development of AI-specific regulations will be crucial for maintaining data security and protecting individual privacy. By staying informed about emerging trends and adhering to best practices, organizations can navigate the complex landscape of data security and build trust with their users.

Chapter 14. The Future of Work and Human-AI Collaboration

The integration of artificial intelligence (AI) into the workforce is revolutionizing how we work, creating new opportunities while also posing potential risks. As AI technologies continue to advance, they are reshaping industries and redefining job roles. This transformation necessitates a rethinking of human-AI collaboration, emphasizing the need for new skills, adaptive work environments, and lifelong learning. In this chapter, we explore the emerging job roles that are being created in the AI era, the opportunities and risks of human-AI synergy, and the importance of continuous learning and adaptation.

Emerging Job Roles in the AI Era

The rise of AI has led to the creation of new and specialized job roles. While some traditional jobs are being automated, AI is also opening up a wide range of opportunities that require human oversight, creativity, and ethical considerations. Understanding these emerging roles can help workers and organizations prepare for the future of work.

AI Specialists and Developers - As AI becomes more embedded in everyday life, there is a growing demand for professionals who can build, implement, and maintain AI systems. Roles such as AI engineers, machine learning specialists, and data scientists are at the forefront of this technological revolution. These experts are responsible for developing algorithms, designing models, and optimizing AI systems to improve performance and efficiency. They also play a crucial role in ensuring that AI systems are ethical and unbiased. AI specialists often work in industries such as healthcare, finance, and autonomous vehicles, where precision and reliability are critical.

- **Skills Required**: A strong background in mathematics, programming languages like Python, and a deep understanding of machine learning algorithms are essential. AI specialists also need problem-solving skills and the ability to work with large datasets.
- **Example**: In the healthcare industry, AI engineers develop algorithms that assist doctors in diagnosing diseases more accurately by analyzing medical images and patient data. In finance, data scientists use AI models to predict market trends and optimize investment strategies.

Data Analysts and Data Ethicists - The value of data has skyrocketed with the advent of AI, making data analysts essential for extracting meaningful insights. Data analysts collect, clean, and interpret data, transforming raw information into actionable knowledge. They work closely with AI teams to ensure that data-driven decisions are well-informed and accurate. On the ethical front, data ethicists are becoming increasingly important. Their role is to address the moral and ethical implications of data collection and usage. They ensure that AI systems are designed and deployed in ways that respect privacy, promote fairness, and are transparent.

- **Skills Required**: Data analysts need strong analytical skills, proficiency in data visualization tools, and knowledge of statistical methods. Data ethicists, on the other hand, require a background in ethics, law, and data privacy, along with the ability to analyze the impact of AI on society.
- **Example**: A data ethicist may work with a tech company to ensure that an AI-powered hiring algorithm does not discriminate against candidates based on race, gender, or socioeconomic background.

AI Trainers and Human-AI Interaction Specialists - AI systems often require human trainers to improve their accuracy and effectiveness. AI trainers are responsible for curating datasets and providing feedback to AI models, teaching them to recognize speech patterns, understand natural language, or identify objects in images. Human-AI interaction specialists, meanwhile, focus on designing intuitive user interfaces that make it easy for people to interact with AI systems. They ensure that AI is user-friendly and accessible, with a focus on enhancing the user experience.

- **Skills Required**: AI trainers need to be detail-oriented and have an understanding of how AI models learn. Human-AI interaction specialists require skills in user experience (UX) design, psychology, and human-computer interaction.

- **Example**: An AI trainer may work with a virtual assistant like Siri or Alexa, teaching it to understand various accents and dialects. A human-AI interaction specialist might design an interface for an AI-powered customer service chatbot, making sure that users can easily get the help they need.

Roles Focused on AI Maintenance and Oversight - As AI becomes more integrated into daily operations, roles focused on monitoring and maintaining AI systems are essential. AI auditors and compliance officers are responsible for ensuring that AI systems adhere to regulatory and ethical standards. They conduct regular audits to check for biases, performance issues, and security vulnerabilities. AI safety engineers work to prevent AI systems from causing unintended harm, whether due to technical errors or incorrect decision-making. Their work ensures that AI systems remain reliable and safe.

- **Skills Required**: These roles require a deep understanding of AI systems, risk assessment, regulatory knowledge, and the ability to conduct thorough audits.
- **Example**: An AI auditor might evaluate a credit scoring algorithm to ensure that it does not unfairly disadvantage certain groups. An AI safety engineer could work on self-driving car systems, making sure they respond appropriately in emergency situations.

These emerging job roles underscore the need for a diverse and skilled workforce capable of working alongside AI and managing its complexities. While AI may automate some routine tasks, it also creates new and meaningful career opportunities that require human oversight and innovation.

Human-AI Synergy: Opportunities and Risks

The collaboration between humans and AI, known as human-AI synergy, has the potential to transform work in profound ways. This partnership leverages the strengths of both humans and machines: AI's ability to process and analyze large datasets and humans' capacity for creativity, critical thinking, and empathy. However, human-AI synergy also comes with risks that need to be carefully managed.

Opportunities in Human-AI Collaboration

1. **Increased Productivity**: One of the most significant advantages of human-AI collaboration is the potential for increased productivity. AI systems can automate repetitive and labor-intensive tasks, allowing human workers to focus on more complex, strategic, and creative work. For example, in the healthcare sector, AI can analyze medical images for signs of disease, enabling radiologists to review cases more quickly and accurately. In manufacturing, robots equipped with AI can perform assembly line tasks, while human workers oversee quality control and make decisions that require human judgment.

   ○ **Example**: In agriculture, AI-powered drones can monitor crop health, allowing farmers to make data-driven decisions about irrigation and pest control. This not only saves time but also increases agricultural productivity.

2. **Enhanced Decision-Making**: AI systems can analyze enormous amounts of data to provide insights that support human decision-making. By identifying patterns and making predictions, AI helps workers make more informed choices. In finance, for instance, AI models can analyze market trends to guide investment strategies, while in urban planning, AI can

model traffic patterns to optimize city infrastructure. Human intuition and experience, combined with AI's analytical power, lead to more effective and efficient decision-making.

- ○ **Example:** In disaster response, AI can analyze satellite imagery to identify areas most in need of assistance, helping emergency responders prioritize resources. Human teams then use this information to make real-time decisions and coordinate relief efforts.

3. **Innovation and Creativity**: AI can act as a powerful tool for enhancing human creativity. In fields like art, design, and engineering, AI-powered software can generate ideas or suggest solutions that humans may not have considered. For example, architects can use AI to create innovative building designs, and musicians can collaborate with AI to compose unique pieces of music. In scientific research, AI accelerates discoveries by analyzing complex datasets and proposing hypotheses.

- ○ **Example:** Pharmaceutical companies use AI to identify potential drug candidates, significantly speeding up the drug discovery process. Researchers then conduct experiments and refine the findings, combining human expertise with AI's data-crunching capabilities.

Risks of Human-AI Collaboration

1. **Job Displacement and Workforce Inequality**: While AI creates new job opportunities, it also has the potential to displace workers in certain industries, particularly in roles that involve routine and repetitive tasks. This can lead to workforce inequality if displaced workers are not provided with opportunities to reskill or transition into new roles. Sectors such as manufacturing, retail, and transportation are particularly vulnerable to job losses due to automation.

Ensuring that workers have access to retraining programs and support is essential for minimizing the negative impact of job displacement.

2. **Bias and Ethical Concerns**: AI systems can unintentionally perpetuate biases present in their training data, leading to unfair or discriminatory outcomes. In collaborative settings, humans may unknowingly rely on biased AI recommendations, which can reinforce existing inequalities. Addressing these biases requires continuous monitoring and ethical oversight. Additionally, there is a risk that humans may become over-reliant on AI, trusting its decisions without sufficient scrutiny, which can have serious consequences.

3. **Privacy and Security Risks**: Human-AI collaboration often involves the exchange of sensitive data, raising concerns about data privacy and security. If AI systems are not properly secured, they can be vulnerable to hacking, data breaches, or misuse. This is particularly concerning in sectors like healthcare and finance, where the protection of personal information is crucial. Organizations must implement stringent data protection measures to safeguard user privacy.

These risks highlight the importance of creating a balanced approach to human-AI collaboration. Organizations must invest in ethical AI practices, provide training and support for workers, and establish clear guidelines for the responsible use of AI.

Lifelong Learning and AI Adaptation

As AI continues to evolve and reshape the job market, the concept of lifelong learning has become more important than ever. Lifelong learning refers to the continuous development of skills and knowledge throughout a person's career. In the AI era, adapting to new technologies and embracing a culture of constant learning are essential for staying relevant and competitive.

The Need for Lifelong Learning - AI and automation are rapidly transforming the skills required in the workplace. Workers must be able to adapt to these changes by learning new technologies, methodologies, and approaches. For example, professionals in fields like marketing may need to learn how to use AI tools for data analysis, while healthcare workers might need to understand how AI assists in diagnostics and treatment planning. The ability to learn and apply new skills will be a key determinant of success in an AI-driven job market.

- **Reskilling and Upskilling**: Reskilling refers to teaching workers entirely new skills so they can transition into different roles, while upskilling focuses on enhancing existing skills to stay current in their field. Companies are increasingly investing in reskilling and upskilling programs to help employees navigate the changes brought about by AI. Governments and educational institutions are also playing a role by offering training programs and certifications in AI and related fields.

Example: A manufacturing worker whose job is automated by AI-powered robotics may be reskilled to take on a role in AI system maintenance or quality assurance. A software developer may upskill by learning about AI and machine learning to design more intelligent applications.

Adapting Education Systems - Traditional education systems must also adapt to prepare students for a future where AI is ubiquitous. This means integrating technology and data literacy into curricula and teaching students how to work alongside AI systems. Schools and universities are starting to offer courses in AI ethics, programming, and human-computer interaction to equip students with the skills they need. Emphasizing critical thinking, creativity, and problem-solving will be crucial, as these are areas where humans excel compared to machines.

- **Example**: Universities are offering interdisciplinary programs that combine computer science with fields like psychology and ethics to train the next generation of AI professionals. These programs teach students how to build AI systems that are not only technically sound but also socially responsible.

The Role of Organizations in Lifelong Learning

Employers have a significant role to play in fostering a culture of lifelong learning. Companies can provide access to online courses, workshops, and mentoring programs that help employees develop new skills. Encouraging a growth mindset and rewarding continuous learning can motivate workers to embrace change rather than fear it. Organizations that prioritize learning and development are better positioned to adapt to technological advancements and remain competitive.

- **Mentorship and Collaboration**: Mentorship programs can facilitate knowledge transfer between experienced employees and those who are newer to the field. Collaborative learning environments, where employees work together to solve problems using AI tools, can also enhance skill development. For instance, a marketing team might collaborate on a project using AI-driven analytics to better understand consumer behavior and optimize campaigns.

Challenges and Barriers to Lifelong Learning - While lifelong learning is essential, there are several challenges that need to be addressed. Not all workers have equal access to training opportunities, especially those in low-income or marginalized communities. Bridging the digital divide and ensuring that everyone has access to the resources they need is crucial for an inclusive AI future. Additionally, older workers may face barriers to learning new technologies, and organizations must find ways to support them, such as offering flexible and tailored training programs.

- **Example**: Governments can offer subsidized training programs and initiatives to help workers transition into new roles, particularly in regions where industries are heavily affected by automation. Public-private partnerships can also be established to expand access to AI education and training.

Lifelong learning is not just about technical skills; it also involves developing soft skills, such as adaptability, emotional intelligence, and ethical reasoning. As AI continues to change the nature of work, the ability to learn and grow will be a crucial asset for individuals and organizations alike.

Summary of Chapter 14

The future of work in the AI era is defined by the emergence of new job roles, the potential for human-AI synergy, and the need for lifelong learning and adaptation. AI is transforming the job market, creating opportunities for AI specialists, data ethicists, and human-AI interaction experts, while also automating routine tasks. Human-AI collaboration offers significant benefits, such as increased productivity and enhanced decision-making, but it also comes with risks, including job displacement, bias, and privacy concerns.

To thrive in an AI-driven world, individuals must embrace lifelong learning, continuously updating their skills to stay relevant. Educational systems, companies, and governments must work together to provide accessible training opportunities and support a culture of continuous learning. By balancing innovation with human values and fostering collaboration between people and machines, we can create a future of work that is both productive and inclusive.

Chapter 15. Conclusion: Navigating the Algorithmic Era

The algorithmic era has transformed the way we live, work, and interact with the world around us. Artificial intelligence (AI) and algorithms have become central to decision-making processes in healthcare, education, finance, and even our daily routines. While AI brings immense potential for growth and innovation, it also presents ethical, societal, and economic challenges that require thoughtful and responsible management. This concluding chapter reflects on the most important takeaways from our exploration of AI, provides strategies for preparing for an AI-driven future, and considers the long-term implications of AI's integration into society.

Key Takeaways from the Algorithmic Integration

The integration of AI and algorithms into various aspects of life has provided numerous benefits, but it has also raised important questions and challenges. As we reflect on the key takeaways from the journey through AI, several themes emerge that are crucial for understanding and navigating the algorithmic era.

AI's Transformative Potential - One of the most significant takeaways is the incredible potential AI has to transform industries and improve quality of life. AI is revolutionizing healthcare by enabling early detection of diseases through advanced imaging analysis and predictive modeling. In the realm of transportation, AI-powered self-driving cars are being developed to reduce traffic accidents and improve efficiency. In education, AI systems provide personalized learning experiences tailored to individual student needs, making education more accessible and effective. The transformative potential of AI lies in its ability to process vast amounts of data, automate routine tasks, and deliver insights that were previously unattainable.

However, with this transformative power comes the need for responsible implementation. AI must be used in ways that genuinely improve lives while minimizing risks and unintended consequences. This requires a comprehensive understanding of AI's capabilities and limitations.

Ethical and Societal Considerations - Another critical takeaway is the need to prioritize ethical and societal considerations in AI development and deployment. AI systems have been shown to reflect and even amplify biases present in their training data, leading to unfair or discriminatory outcomes. For instance, biased algorithms used in hiring processes may disadvantage certain demographic groups, while biased facial recognition systems can lead to higher rates of misidentification for people of color. Addressing these issues requires a commitment to ethical practices, such as fairness, transparency, and accountability.

Moreover, data privacy is a significant concern in an era where AI systems collect and analyze massive amounts of personal information. Ensuring that individuals have control over their data and that AI systems operate in a transparent manner is essential for building trust and protecting human rights. Ethical guidelines and oversight mechanisms must be developed to address these challenges and ensure that AI serves the common good.

The Power of Human-AI Collaboration - Human-AI collaboration is another key theme that has emerged from the integration of AI into our world. While AI excels at processing information, recognizing patterns, and making predictions, it lacks the human qualities of creativity, empathy, and moral reasoning. By combining AI's strengths with human skills, we can achieve better outcomes in many areas. For example, AI can assist doctors in diagnosing illnesses, but the compassionate care and nuanced understanding provided by human doctors remain irreplaceable. Similarly, AI can help businesses optimize operations, but strategic decisions still require human judgment.

The future of work will be shaped by this collaboration between humans and AI, emphasizing the need for workers to develop new skills and adapt to changing job roles. Human-AI collaboration presents both opportunities and challenges, but with the right approach, it can lead to a more innovative and efficient world.

Preparing for an AI-Driven Future

As AI continues to evolve, preparing for an AI-driven future requires proactive efforts from individuals, organizations, and governments. Embracing change, promoting continuous learning, and ensuring equitable access to technology are essential steps for successfully navigating the AI landscape.

Education and Lifelong Learning - One of the most critical strategies for preparing for an AI-driven future is investing in education and lifelong learning. The rapid pace of technological change means that workers will need to continually update their skills to remain competitive. Traditional education systems must adapt to teach students not only technical skills like programming and data analysis but also critical thinking, problem-solving, and ethical reasoning. Courses on AI ethics, machine learning, and data privacy should become standard in school curricula to prepare students for the challenges and opportunities they will face.

Lifelong learning is also crucial for workers already in the workforce. Reskilling and upskilling programs can help employees transition into new roles created by AI or enhance their existing skills. Companies should invest in training initiatives that teach employees how to work effectively with AI tools. For example, a marketing professional might learn how to use AI for data-driven campaign analysis, while a healthcare worker might be trained to interpret AI-generated diagnostic insights.

- **Example**: Governments and organizations can offer free or subsidized online courses in AI and data science, making education accessible to a broader audience. Collaboration between educational institutions and the tech industry can ensure that training programs are relevant and up to date.

Policy and Regulation - Governments play a crucial role in shaping an AI-driven future by enacting policies and regulations that protect citizens and promote fairness. Data privacy laws, like the General Data Protection Regulation (GDPR) in the European Union, set important precedents for how personal information should be handled. Similar regulatory frameworks are needed to address issues specific to AI, such as the ethical use of facial recognition technology or the accountability of AI-driven decision-making systems.

Policymakers must work with industry leaders, ethicists, and the public to develop regulations that strike a balance between innovation and safety. International cooperation is also essential, as AI is a global technology that transcends borders. Establishing global standards for AI ethics and governance can ensure that AI is developed and used responsibly worldwide.

- **Example**: Policymakers can create AI ethics boards that oversee the deployment of AI in public services, ensuring that algorithms are transparent, unbiased, and fair. Countries can collaborate on international treaties that set guidelines for the ethical use of AI, particularly in sensitive areas like military applications or cross-border data sharing.

Investing in Human-AI Collaboration - Organizations must invest in tools and practices that support effective human-AI collaboration. This includes designing AI systems that are user-friendly and intuitive, so that people can easily interact with and benefit from AI technology. It also means fostering a culture of innovation where employees are encouraged to view AI as a partner rather than a competitor. Companies can create interdisciplinary teams that include AI specialists, ethicists, and domain experts to ensure that AI solutions are well-rounded and impactful.

- **Example**: In the retail industry, AI can be used to optimize inventory management, but human employees are needed to provide personalized customer service and handle complex situations. Training programs that teach workers how to use AI tools can help them become more effective in their roles and open up new opportunities for growth.

Preparing for an AI-driven future is a shared responsibility that requires collaboration between governments, businesses, and individuals. By investing in education, enacting thoughtful policies, and fostering human-AI collaboration, we can create a future where AI enhances rather than diminishes human potential.

Reflecting on AI's Long-Term Implications

As we look ahead to the future, it is essential to consider the long-term implications of AI on society, the economy, and the human experience. The choices we make today in designing and deploying AI technologies will shape the world for future generations, and careful reflection is needed to ensure positive outcomes.

Impact on Employment and the Economy - AI has already begun to reshape the job market, automating certain roles while creating new opportunities. In the long term, AI is expected to boost economic productivity and spur innovation. However, this shift may also widen economic disparities if job displacement is not managed effectively. Workers whose roles are automated may struggle to find new employment if they do not have access to reskilling programs. Addressing these challenges requires forward-thinking policies that provide safety nets and retraining opportunities for affected workers.

- **Example**: Automation in manufacturing could lead to significant job losses, but at the same time, it could create new roles in AI system maintenance, robotics engineering, and data analysis. Governments must invest in workforce development programs to help workers transition into these new careers.

Social and Ethical Considerations - The widespread use of AI will also have long-term social and ethical implications. AI systems that influence healthcare, education, and criminal justice must be designed with fairness and accountability in mind. If left unchecked, biases in AI algorithms could exacerbate existing social inequalities and erode public trust in technology. Reflecting on these ethical concerns and prioritizing human rights will be crucial as AI continues to evolve.

- **Example**: AI-driven predictive policing algorithms have raised concerns about racial bias and unjust targeting of minority communities. Ensuring that such systems are transparent and subject to oversight can mitigate these risks and promote more just outcomes.

AI's Influence on Human Interaction and Society - AI is also changing the way humans interact with each other and society as a whole. The increasing presence of AI in our daily lives can have profound effects on social behaviors, relationships, and even our sense of identity. For example, social media platforms use AI algorithms to curate content and influence what information people see, shaping opinions and reinforcing echo chambers. In the long term, this could contribute to greater social polarization if not managed carefully.

Moreover, as AI systems become more human-like, such as virtual companions and AI-driven customer service agents, there is a risk that people may become more isolated from genuine human interaction. While AI can provide convenience and efficiency, it cannot fully replace the emotional depth and complexity of human relationships. Reflecting on how AI affects our social fabric is essential to ensure that technology enhances rather than diminishes human connections.

AI and the Future of Creativity and Innovation - Another long-term implication of AI is its impact on human creativity and innovation. AI has already shown its potential to assist in creative processes, such as composing music, writing stories, and generating artwork. In scientific research, AI helps analyze data and generate hypotheses, accelerating discoveries in fields like medicine and climate science. However, there are questions about whether AI will eventually surpass human creativity or, conversely, limit the scope of human expression by becoming a dominant creative force.

The future will likely see a blend of human and AI-driven creativity, where AI acts as a collaborator rather than a replacement for human ingenuity. The challenge lies in finding the right balance and ensuring that AI is used as a tool to empower, rather than overshadow, human creativity.

The Ethical and Philosophical Questions of AI

AI also raises deep philosophical questions about the nature of consciousness, autonomy, and what it means to be human. As AI systems become more advanced and capable of performing tasks that were once thought to require human intelligence, society will need to grapple with questions about the rights and responsibilities of AI entities. Should highly advance AI systems have any form of legal status? How do we ensure that AI aligns with human values in a world that is rapidly changing?

These questions do not have easy answers, but they underscore the importance of continued ethical reflection and dialogue. Philosophers, ethicists, technologists, and the general public must work together to navigate the complexities of AI and make informed decisions about its role in society.

Summary of Chapter 15

Navigating the algorithmic era requires a thoughtful and balanced approach. The integration of AI into society has the potential to revolutionize industries, improve quality of life, and unlock new avenues for innovation. However, it also raises ethical, social, and economic challenges that must be carefully managed. The key takeaways from AI integration emphasize the importance of ethical considerations, the power of human-AI collaboration, and the need for continuous learning and adaptation.

Preparing for an AI-driven future involves investing in education, enacting policies that protect individuals and promote fairness, and fostering environments where humans and AI can work together harmoniously. Reflecting on AI's long-term implications reminds us that the choices we make today will shape the future of our society. By prioritizing human values, promoting responsible innovation, and maintaining a commitment to fairness and equity, we can harness the power of AI to create a more just, inclusive, and thriving world.

Milton Keynes UK
Ingram Content Group UK Ltd.
UKHW042032031224
452078UK00001B/79

9 798230 882664